LCVP Student Record Book for Link Modules

Deirdre McGarry

Gill & Macmillan

Gill & Macmillan Ltd
Hume Avenue
Park West
Dublin 12
with associated companies throughout the world
www.gillmacmillan.ie

© Deirdre McGarry 2006
ISBN-13: 978 07171 4002 2
ISBN-10: 0 7171 4002 4
Print origination in Ireland by Designit

The paper used in this book is made from the wood pulp of managed forests. For every tree felled, at least one tree is planted, thereby renewing natural resources.

All rights reserved.
No part of this publication may be copied, reproduced or transmitted in any form or by any means without written permission of the publishers or else under the terms of any licence permitting limited copying issued by the Irish Copyright Licensing Agency.

Contents

Introduction	1
Link Module 1: Preparation for the world of work	5
Unit 1: Introduction to working life	6
Unit 2: Job-seeking skills	45
Unit 3: Career investigation	70
Unit 4: Work placement	98
Link Module 2: Enterprise education	119
Unit 5: Enterprise skills	120
Unit 6: Local business enterprises	153
Unit 7: Local voluntary organisations and community enterprises	186
Unit 8: An enterprise activity	223
Exam terms	264

Introduction

The Leaving Certificate Vocational Programme (LCVP) was introduced to enhance the vocational dimension of the established Leaving Certificate. The programme puts a strong focus on self-directed learning, enterprise, work and the community.

Requirements for the Leaving Certificate Vocational Programme, which is of two years' duration, are as follows:

- LCVP students must take a minimum of five Leaving Certificate Subjects (at Higher, Ordinary or Foundation Level) including Irish.
- Two of the above must be selected from one of the designated Vocational Subject groupings (these are groups of Leaving Certificate subjects which link naturally together). These listings are sent by the Department of Education to schools annually.
- Students must follow a recognised course in a modern European language (other than Irish or English).
- They must study two additional Link Modules, *Preparation for the world of work* and *Enterprise education*.

PREPARATION FOR THE WORLD OF WORK

Research and investigate local employment opportunities; develop your job-seeking skills, such as letter writing, CV presentation, interview techniques; gain valuable practical experience of the world of work; interview and work-shadow a person in a career area that interests you.

ENTERPRISE EDUCATION

Organise study visits to local business and community enterprises; meet and interview enterprising people on-site and in the classroom; plan and undertake interesting activities that will build self-confidence and creativity and initiative and develop your teamwork, communication and computer skills.

The *Link Modules* are activity-based units of study which are designed to help students make connections between school and community, study and future career, enterprise and the business of making a living. LCVP students follow the same subject syllabi and are assessed in the same way as their peers in the Leaving Certificate.

The Link Modules are assessed by:

WRITTEN EXAMINATION (40%)	PORTFOLIO OF COURSE WORK (60%)
This examination takes place in May of your Leaving Certificate year. It takes two and a half hours. It is composed of: • audio visual section • case study (sent to schools one month prior to exam) • general question (four from six)	This portfolio is sent to the Department of Education with your written exam. The portfolio should be based on the numerous activities you took part in over the two-year programme. **Core items:** • curriculum vitae • career investigation • summary report • enterprise/action plan **Optional items:** (two from four) • diary of work experience • enterprise report • recorded interview/presentation • report on 'My Own Place'

No two portfolio items should be on the same activity (with the exception of the Enterprise Plan and Enterprise Report).

Note: teachers should also refer to guidelines on assessment arrangements issued to schools from time to time by the examining board.

Examination questions and portfolio items are included throughout this book.

LCVP promotes active learning. For active learning to be effective, students should take ownership of the activities they have selected. It is by taking responsibility for their own learning that students grow in the qualities and skills of personal enterprise. Every activity students engage in should be broken down into five distinct phases: planning, the experience, de-briefing, evaluation and recording.

Grades and points awarded for the Link Modules
Distinction (80–100 per cent)   70 points
Merit (65–79 per cent)   50 points
Pass (50–64 per cent)   30 points
The Link Modules are recognised in points terms by institutes of technology and by universities.

To the teacher
I hope you find this book useful and that it becomes a resource that you or your students will not be without. May it ease your use of the photocopier and help make your job that little bit easier.

To the student
May you enjoy the LCVP experience of active learning. Make the most of this great opportunity and participate in all activities. I hope this book will help you in your studies, activities and portfolio preparation.

With thanks

I would like to take this opportunity to thank all the people who supported me and this Record Book. The LCVP team I work with, who added to these resources: Úna McNulty, Sinead McGarvey, Erica Farrell and Anne Robinson. The LCVP students whom I have taught (and teach): they have inspired me. Thanks to the LCVP Support Services for allowing use of material and resources. Thanks to Celine Doohan for guidance. Most of all, my family, Saoirse and Caitriona, for time, patience and silence.

Link Module 1
Preparation for the World of Work

Unit 1 — Introduction to working life

The aim of this unit is to encourage and facilitate young people to find out for themselves as much as possible about working life and local employment opportunities. The term 'working life' is used here in the broadest sense to include paid employment and unpaid voluntary work. Many of the learning outcomes of this unit may be achieved by students engaging in a local study of 'My Own Place'. This unit should be integrated with Units 6 and 7 of Link Module 2: Enterprise Education .

SPECIFIC LEARNING OUTCOMES
The student should be able to

1.1	identify the main sources of employment in the local area	p. 27
1.2	identify the main social services and job creation agencies in the local area	pp. 15, 28
1.3	identify the main agencies that provide transport in the local area	p. 26
1.4	identify the main financial institutions servicing the needs of the local area	p. 26
1.5	identify the main agencies involved in industrial relations in the local area	p. 26
1.6	identify the principal economic activities of the local area	p. 27
1.7	evaluate the potential for tourism in the local area	p. 27
1.8	identify and understand the main differences between school and work	pp. 10–11
1.9	describe the intrinsic value of various forms of work including self-employment and voluntary work	pp. 7, 8, 9
1.10	understand current regulations/legislation relating to the employment of young workers	p. 10
1.11	understand current health and safety regulations in workplaces	pp. 11, 12
1.12	role-play a situation that could give rise to a dispute in the workplace	p. 14
1.13	understand issues related to diversity in the workplace	pp. 14, 15
1.14	list the different forms of assistance for unemployed people	pp. 15, 16
1.15	arrange a visit to a training scheme in the locality and/or invite an appropriate speaker from such an organisation to visit the group in the school	pp. 16, 17 18,19
1.16	link the activities in this unit to learning in relevant Leaving Certificate subjects.	pp. 43, 44

EMPLOYMENT

There are a number of different types of paid employment that you can engage in.

Full-time employment

Most full-time permanent employees work between thirty-eight to forty hours per week on a regular, on-going basis.

Part-time employment

Part-time employees work on a regular, on-going basis but work fewer hours than full-time employees.

Casual employment

Casual workers are on standby to do work as required without fixed hours or attendance arrangements.

Fixed-term employment

Fixed-term employees are employed to do a job for an agreed length of time. Many employers hire fixed-term employees to work on a specific project or to fill in for employees who may be on leave.

Identify advantages of paid employment:

ADVANTAGES OF EMPLOYMENT
1 **Regular income**
2
3
4
5

Self-employment

There is no employer; self-employed people work for themselves. They control the work and their conditions. They pay themselves out of any profits made.

Identify advantages and disadvantages of self-employment:

ADVANTAGES AND DISADVANTAGES OF SELF-EMPLOYMENT	
Advantages	**Disadvantages**
1 You are your own boss	1 Long working hours
2	2
3	3
4	4
5	5

VOLUNTARY WORK

Not all work is paid employment. Some people work for reasons other than financial reward; they want to provide our communities with a service. There are examples of these people all around us.

Charity organisations
- St Vincent de Paul
- Alone
- Red Cross

Community groups
- youth club leaders
- girl guides
- scouts
- sporting groups: GAA, soccer clubs, basketball clubs etc.
- residents' associations

Why do people do voluntary work?

WHAT MOTIVATES PEOPLE TO DO VOLUNTARY WORK?
1
2
3

Identify voluntary groups in your area:

VOLUNTARY GROUPS IN YOUR AREA
1
2
3
4
5

YOUNG PEOPLE AND EMPLOYMENT

Many of you will have engaged in work. However are you aware that the law protects you? *The Protection of Young Persons (Employment) Act 1996* was introduced to protect young workers in Ireland. It ensures that work carried out during your very important school years does not put your education at risk.

The Act sets:

- minimum age limits for employment
- break times
- maximum number of working hours
- late-night work

Maximum weekly working hours for young people under sixteen

Age	14	15
School term-time	nil	8 hours
Work experience	40 hours	40 hours
Working hours	not before 8 a.m., not after 8 p.m.	

Working hours, time off and rest breaks for young people aged sixteen and seventeen

MAXIMUM WORKING DAY	8 hours
MAXIMUM WORKING WEEK	40 hours
HALF-HOUR REST BREAK AFTER	4½ hours' work
DAILY REST BREAK	12 consecutive hours off
WEEKLY REST BREAK	2 days off, to be consecutive as far as is practicable
WORKING HOURS	Not before 6 a.m., not after 10 p.m.

Minimum wage for young people

While there is a national minimum wage in Ireland, young people who are under eighteen are only guaranteed up to seventy per cent of the national minimum wage. Your employer may pay you more than the minimum wage, but they are not required to do so by law.

Difference between work and school

Are there differences between school and work? Of course there are. Many of these differences are obvious (pay) however others may require some thought. List your top five differences below then discuss these differences as a class.

MY TOP FIVE DIFFERENCES BETWEEN SCHOOL AND WORK
1
2
3
4
5

HEALTH AND SAFETY REGULATIONS

Your health, safety and welfare in the workplace is protected by:
- **Safety, Health and Welfare at Work Act 1989**
- **Safety, Health and Welfare at Work Regulations 1993**

They outline the obligations of the employer and the employee.

Obligations of the employer

- Prepare a safety statement for the workplace identifying any hazards or risks and how they should be dealt with.
- Inform employees of the protective equipment (clothing etc.) required for the job, provide such equipment and train employees in its use.
- Provide a safe working environment.
- Protect employees using visual display units (VDUs, computer screens) by examining the glare on the screen and the employee's position relative to the VDU. Arrange for employees to take regular eye tests and contribute to the cost of prescription eyewear.
- Document in detail all reports of accidents in the workplace.
- Protect pregnant employees.
- Pay health and safety leave (normal wage) to employees who are eligible, for up to three weeks.

- Provide a procedure for dealing with bullying.
- Put in place safeguards to eliminate the risk of violence. Provide employees with appropriate means of minimising risk, for example, security glass.

Obligations of the employee
- Obtain a copy of the safety statement. Employees should read it and make sure they understand it.
- Take reasonable care and use the protective equipment supplied by the employer.
- Report all accidents to the employer.
- Respect co-workers, do not discriminate against or bully others.

Get a copy of your school's or your part-time job's safety statement. Copy down the main points in the box below.

SAFETY STATEMENT

INDUSTRIAL RELATIONS
People involved in industrial relations
- employer
- Irish Business Employers Confederation (IBEC) – interest group that lobbies on behalf of employers
- employee(s)
- shop steward – represents employees in the workplace on behalf of their trade union
- trade union – looks after the interests of employees and represents them during industrial conflict. *Examples:* SIPTU: Services, Industrial, Professional and Technical Union; ASTI: Association of Secondary Teachers in Ireland
- Irish Congress of Trade Unions (ICTU) – interest group that lobbies on behalf of trade unions

Causes of conflict
In every workplace there will be some degree of industrial conflict. The main causes of conflict in the workplace include:
- different objectives: different people in the workplace want different things out of a task
- communication problems: unclear messages given to people, people not given enough time to do a task, people not using appropriate language etc.
- leadership style: people do not like to be dictated to and if a manager is autocratic (dictates to staff) there can be industrial unrest
- availability of resources: resources required for a job not being made available to staff
- promotion: people feeling they deserve a promotion more than their co-workers

CAN YOU IDENTIFY ANY OTHER CAUSES OF CONFLICT?
1
2

Dealing with conflict
There are several steps to be taken when dealing with conflict:

Step 1: Talk it out. The two groups involved in the conflict should sit down informally and talk about what has happened.

Step 2: Negotiate. This is more formal than step 1 and can often involve the shop steward's stepping in to assist the employee in talks. Negotiation between trade unions and employers about wages and work conditions is called collective bargaining.

Step 3: Conciliation. Here a third party will sit in and listen to discussions between the parties involved in the dispute. They will offer advice that can be accepted or rejected by those involved. *Examples:* Labour Relations Commission (where a group of employees is involved); Rights Commissioner (where an individual is taking a case against an employer).

Step 4: Arbitration. This also involves the intervention of a third party; however, this time both parties in the dispute agree that the decision of the arbitrator will be accepted (binding). *Example:* The Labour Court.

Read and role play the following case studies and decide what would be the best method to solve each conflict:

CASE STUDY	SOLUTION
Manager has denied an employee a request for a personal day	
Employees have been unfairly selected for redundancy	
Employee is being bullied by another employee	
Employees want more wages	

DIVERSITY IN THE WORKPLACE

We are all different and in the workplace there are lots of different groups of people. Whoever you are you deserve to be treated with respect and equality.

The Employment Equality Acts 1998 and 2004 deal with discrimination in employment. The Acts deal with discrimination related to any of the following nine grounds:

- gender
- marital status
- family status
- age
- race
- religion
- disability
- sexual orientation
- membership of the travelling community

Employment issues dealt with by the Acts include:
- **dismissal**
- **equal pay**
- **harassment and sexual harassment**
- **working conditions**
- **promotion**
- **access to employment etc.**

All disputes must relate to one or more of the nine grounds listed above.

ASSISTANCE FOR UNEMPLOYED PEOPLE

Financial support
Department of Social and Family Affairs
Provides weekly unemployment benefit/assistance. To qualify for this financial assistance you must be:
- **unemployed**
- **under sixty-six years of age**
- **capable of work**
- **available for full-time work**
- **genuinely seeking work**

Training support
Department of Social and Family Affairs
The Department of Social and Family Affairs, with other agencies, administers training and educational options. These schemes are designed to bridge the gap between welfare dependency and employment by helping people with the often difficult transition between the two. *Examples:*
- **Part-time Job Incentive Scheme**
- **Vocational Training Opportunities Scheme**

FÁS
FÁS is Ireland's national training and employment authority. It aims to:
- **improve employability**
- **meet labour market needs**
- **promote social inclusion**

FÁS offers a wide range of courses including:
- **community employment schemes**
- **day and evening courses**
- **apprenticeship schemes**
- **environmental training courses**
- **FÁS Net College**

Youthreach

Youthreach is aimed at people between the ages of fifteen and twenty who have left school without any formal training. It aims to improve vocational and work experience skills.

Fáilte Ireland

Fáilte supports the development of the Irish tourist industry by developing skills in the tourism and catering sector. Fáilte Ireland offers a range of full-time and part-time courses.

Coillte

Coillte works closely with those involved in timber production and provides services in Ireland in the areas of forestry. Coillte provides training for those interested in entering this profession.

The Crafts Council of Ireland

The Crafts Council aims to develop the market for Irish craft at home and abroad. It runs full-time craft-related training courses in jewellery and pottery.

Identify a training centre in your area:

_____

Research information about this training centre or scheme on the Internet (or by phone if the internet is not available) and answer the following questions:

Postal address of training centre

_____

_____

E-mail address of training centre

_____

Phone number of training centre

_____

Contact name in training centre

_____

How does this centre help local people in your area?

_____

_____

_____

Call a meeting

As a class you are now going to organise a visit to, or a visitor from the training centre. In order to organise this activity you will need to call a class meeting. The roles of people in a meeting are detailed on page 134.

Agenda

Every meeting requires an agenda (items to be discussed). Examples of items on the agenda could include:
- **permission for the visit**
- **date for the visit**
- **delegation of jobs for the visit, e.g. contact training centre, prepare questions, type questions, organise transport, organise a room etc.**

As a class decide on the agenda for your meeting.

AGENDA
Title:
Date:
Time:
Venue:
Chairperson:
Secretary:
Agenda **Minutes from last meeting**

AOB (Any Other Business)
Signed: **(Secretary)**

Minutes

During the meeting the secretary should keep minutes of every item being discussed. If somebody in the class volunteers to do a job this should be included in the minutes, as should the date they will have their job done by.

MINUTES OF MEETING

Meeting topic:
Date:
Time:
Venue:
Chairperson:
Secretary:
Minutes on each item discussed

Signed: (Secretary)

After you have visited the training centre or invited a speaker in from the centre you should prepare a summary report on the activity.

Portfolio core item

SUMMARY REPORT
(300–600 words)

Prepared by

Title of report
What the report is about.

Terms of reference
Instructions given to you, the report writer, by your teacher.

Aims
Can be used in place of terms of reference.
What you and your class wanted to get from the activity.

Group aims

Individual aims

_____

_____

_____

_____

_____

_____

Body of report

Divide your report into three areas. There must be a logical sequence to summarise your main findings. You may decide to place paragraphs in order of importance or in chronological order, depending on the subject matter of the summary report. The use of numbered or bold headings and bulleted lists is recommended.

Subheading 1

_____

_____

_____

_____

_____

_____

_____

_____

_____

Subheading 2

Subheading 3

Conclusions
Must link with aims and report content.

Group conclusions

_____

_____

_____

_____

Individual conclusions

_____

_____

_____

_____

Recommendations
Suggestions for future action, based on the summary report. Recommendations might also include ideas for follow-on activities or describe how you might perform better in a future exercise.

_____

_____

_____

_____

Signed: _____

This summary report can be submitted as a portfolio item so long as it does not link with any other portfolio item.

> IT: Use a word processing software package (e.g. Microsoft Word) to type up your report. It should be typed in Times New Roman font, size 12. Make headings and subheadings stand out by using **bold** and *italics*.

Evaluate the activity
Personal evaluation
What did you get from this activity? Did you learn information you did not previously know? Did you improve any skills?

_____

_____

_____

_____

Group evaluation
Have a discussion among group members. Did you work well together?

_____

_____

_____

_____

MY OWN PLACE
Investigation of your local area
This research can be used to prepare a report on 'your own place', p. 29.
You are going to investigate your locality. This can be
- **where you go to school**
- **where you live**

Research your locality using the following resources:

- **your own general knowledge**
- **your family's and friends' general knowledge**
- **the internet – your local town will probably have a website**
- **the local telephone directory**
- **local newspapers**
- **the library**

Use the resources named above to answer the following questions:

Name of your local area

_____

Size of the area

_____

Population of the area

_____

Brief history of the area

_____

_____

_____

_____

Sketch a map or find an aerial photo of your area

Identify the main sources of transport in your area

Dart, Luas, airport, sea port, public or private bus, train, taxi, courier

Identify the main financial institutions in your area

Banks, building societies, credit unions

Identify any industrial relations agencies in your area

Trade Unions, ICTU, IBEC

Identify the principal economic activity in your area

LOCAL BUSINESS
Manufacturers
Wholesalers
Retailers
Service providers

Identify the main sources of employment in your area

_____

_____

_____

_____

Identify the main facilities for tourism in your area
Hotels, B&Bs, caravan parks, parks, heritage parks, beach

_____

_____

_____

_____

Could tourism be improved in any way?
Information centre, more accommodation, tidy the town, website highlighting tourist attractions

___

Identify the main social facilities in your area

Children *(playgroups, playgrounds etc.)* **and teenagers** *(youth clubs, discos, sporting pitch etc.):*

Adults *(community centre, public house, leisure centres):*

Elderly *(old people's home, retirement associations, meals on wheels etc.):*

Unemployed *(training centres, housing and community groups):*

Evaluation

IDENTIFY ONE THING YOU HAVE LEARNED FROM THIS ACTIVITY

IDENTIFY A FOLLOW-UP ACTIVITY FROM THIS RESEARCH

Optional portfolio item

Identify one element of your own area that you would like to investigate, such as tourism, a training centre, facilities for the unemployed, transport etc.

REPORT ON 'MY OWN PLACE'
(1000–1500 words)

Title
What the report is about.

Prepared by
Who prepared the report (you).

Table of contents
Fill this in when your report is complete.

Topic	Page number
Summary of report	
Description of local area	
Aims	
Body of report	
Planning	
Research	
Out-of-school activity	
Main findings	
Suggestions for improvements	
My personal contribution	
Conclusion	
Recommendations	
Evaluation	

Summary of contents

*Summary of what this **report** contains – overall view of the work to come.*

Description of the local area

Brief description of the area under investigation (rural/urban area, county name, main roads, distance from capital etc.). You could also include an illustration or a map or photo of the area.

Aims

Personal aims

Group aims

Body of report

Planning

Planning you did for the investigation.

Research

Identify and outline the research methods you used (minimum of two required).

_____

_____

_____

_____

_____

_____

_____

Out-of-school activity
This could take the form of an interview with a relevant local person or a visit to a relevant organisation etc.

Name activity

_____

Details of activity

_____

_____

_____

_____

_____

Main findings

Use a logical sequence. Analyse key findings. You should use illustrations here.

Analysis of one issue
Identify an area that requires improvement and suggest a way this could be done.

Area requiring improvement

Suggested methods of improvement
Examples: contact a TD, form a lobby group etc.

Your personal contribution to the investigation

Conclusion
Link with aims.

Personal conclusions

Group conclusions

Recommendations
Suggestions for future action, based on the summary report. Recommendations might also include ideas for follow-on activities or you could describe how you might perform better in a future exercise.

Evaluation

Personal evaluation

State how this investigation linked with at least two of your LCVP subjects.

Evaluation of investigation

Evaluation of doing the report

Appendices

Up to two appendices can be included, e.g. tables, maps, photos.

This report on my own place can be submitted as a portfolio item so long as it does not link with any other portfolio item.

IT: Use a word processing software package (e.g. Microsoft Word) to type up your report. It should be typed in Times New Roman font, size 12. Make headings and subheadings stand out by using **bold** and *italics*.

Exam questions

Q1.

a) List **three** employers in the area where you go to school. State what type of business organisation they are.

(6 marks)

b) If a person were unable to obtain work, what financial benefit(s) would the state provide?

(4 marks)

c) Describe **one** state scheme in operation to help unemployed people return to work.

(9 marks)

d) School work is a form of work for which you do not receive payment. Name **three** other forms of work.

(6 marks)

Q2.

Everyone is engaged in either paid or unpaid work.

a) Describe **three** benefits (non-financial) to be gained from participation in work.

(6 marks)

b) Identify and explain **four** qualities that help to make a person more employable.

(8 marks)

c) Name **three** financial institutions serving the needs of your local area.

(3 marks)

d) Name and describe in detail **two** different schemes in operation to help unemployed people return to the workforce.

(8 marks)

CASE STUDY
(30 marks)

Rathlee

Rathlee is a rural town situated sixty miles from the nearest city. The facilities and services in the town serve those living there as well as the wider rural area. Rathlee has two second-level schools and a district hospital. A modern shopping centre opened two years ago in the centre of the town. There is also a new cinema complex, a leisure centre and a swimming pool. Many people, most of whom live locally, are employed in the shopping centre.

Rathlee benefits from the tourists that the town attracts. There are a number of important historical monuments nearby and business also comes from guests staying at a recently renovated local hotel. The hotel is an old period building which has been restored and extended to include a conference centre.

There is a well established arts and craft centre in the town. Many craftspeople work in the workshops that are part of the centre. The centre has a thriving retail outlet for the goods produced. A small but successful business park is located on the outskirts of the town. This has attracted industry to the area and has encouraged local people to develop their own businesses or set up new ones.

Local people have watched the town prosper and grow over the last few years. Recently some people have become concerned that while the town has developed there are no facilities or services for the many elderly people living in the town and surrounding countryside.

Ann Smyth and James Lynch live and work in Rathlee. They both know many elderly people living on their own, some in remote parts of the countryside. With a number of other concerned people from the area they have formed a group. The aim of this group is to raise money to build a day care centre for the elderly.

It is hoped that a day care centre would provide activities, services and meals for the elderly. Transport to and from the centre would also have to be provided. Ann and James have formed a committee of six to get this project up and running. They have been joined on the committee by hard-working individuals who in the past have been involved in many local projects such as Tidy Towns and fund-raising for the schools.

The committee began work by preparing a submission on why the day care centre is needed, what is required to get the project up and running and on the operation of the centre once completed. They approached the local health board, which agreed to provide a site for the centre in the grounds of the hospital. They also applied for and were awarded a grant from the national lottery for some funds towards the cost of building the centre. The remaining funds must be raised locally.

The committee has now to decide on appropriate fund-raising activities. The residents in the town and surrounding areas, the business community and local organisations are all supportive of this project. They see it as worthwhile and beneficial to everyone. There are many offers of help.

Q1.

Outline **three** reasons why you might consider moving to Rathlee to live.

(6 marks)

Q2.

a) Why, in your opinion, do Ann and James have a strong sense of commitment to their area?

b) Outline how the wider community can benefit from this.

(12 marks)

UNIT EVALUATION
Did you cover specific learning outcomes?

SPECIFIC LEARNING OUTCOME	COVERED (TICK)
1.1 identify the main sources of employment in the local area	
1.2 identify the main social services and job creation agencies in the local area	
1.3 identify the main agencies that provide transport in the local area	
1.4 identify the main financial institutions servicing the needs of the local area	
1.5 identify the main agencies involved in industrial relations in the local area	
1.6 identify the principal economic activities of the local area	
1.7 evaluate the potential for tourism in the local area	
1.8 identify and understand the main differences between school and work	
1.9 describe the intrinsic value of various forms of work including self-employment and voluntary work	
1.10 understand current regulations/legislation relating to the employment of young workers	
1.11 understand current health and safety regulations in workplaces	
1.12 role-play a situation that could give rise to a dispute in the workplace	
1.13 understand issues related to diversity in the workplace	
1.14 list the different forms of assistance for unemployed people	
1.15 arrange a visit to a training scheme in the locality and/or invite an appropriate speaker from such an organisation to visit the group in the school	
1.16 link the activities in this unit to learning in relevant Leaving Certificate subjects.	

Does this unit and your learning experience link with any other Leaving Certificate subjects?

SUBJECT	HOW IT LINKS

What was your favourite part of this unit and why?

Did you encounter any problems during this unit? How could you overcome these problems in future?

PROBLEM	SOLUTION

Unit 2	Job-seeking skills

The aim of this unit is to equip students with the skills and confidence necessary to gain employment and to develop their organisational and communicative skills. The involvement of adults from business and the local community is recommended in order to help students gain practice in presenting themselves to prospective employers.

SPECIFIC LEARNING OUTCOMES

The student should be able to

2.1	recognise the different ways in which job vacancies are advertised	p. 45
2.2	apply for a job by letter, telephone and e-mail	pp. 45–50
2.3	complete an application form	pp. 50–57
2.4	compile and create a curriculum vitae in word-processed format	pp. 57–62
2.5	explain how to prepare for a job interview	pp. 62–63
2.6	engage in a simulated job interview	pp. 63–64

Ways in which jobs are advertised

Advertising is a method of direct communication with your target market and trying to persuade them to buy your product, use your service or, in this case, apply for a job in your business.

The following are places where advertisements can be placed:

- local and national newspapers
- notice boards
- trade and specialist magazines
- radio
- television and teletext
- the internet – recruitment websites, companies' own websites
- recruitment agencies
- recruitment fairs
- government agencies – FÁS, Cert

Letter-writing

Letter-writing is a very popular method of responding to a job advertisement. The letter should be a summary of why you should be employed.

Writing or typing the letter

- Write a first draft of the letter, using short concise sentences.
- Read over this draft checking for spelling, grammar and punctuation mistakes.
- Edit your first draft.

SUGGESTED LAYOUT FOR A LETTER	SAMPLE LETTER

Your address

Your telephone number
Date

Title of person you are writing to
Address of person you are writing to

Dear Sir/Madam (use name if known),

Paragraph 1:
Introduce yourself and the reason you are writing (one or two sentences).

Paragraph 2:
Highlight your skills, qualities and experiences relevant to the job. (You may require two paragraphs for this.)

Paragraph 3:
Closing paragraph. Make it clear you are available for interview or further questioning. Mention if you have included a copy of your CV.

Closing salutation:
Yours sincerely/faithfully
Your signature – underlined
Your name in print

---

24 Main Street
Balbriggan
Co. Dublin
Tel: 183 6678
8th January 2006

The Manager
Fagan's Supermarket
Dublin Road
Drogheda

Dear Sir/Madam,

I am a 6th year LCVP student at Manor House School, Raheny. I wish to apply for the summer job you have advertised in the local newspaper.

I have excellent communication skills. This will be a huge asset when working in your supermarket and dealing with customers. I would also describe myself as a team player and enjoy working with others.

I have worked in my local newsagents part time while in transition and fifth year. During that time I stacked shelves when required and I worked on the cash register.

I have included a copy of my curriculum vitae for your attention. I am available for interview at any time.

Yours sincerely

Niamh Rourke

Read the following advertisement and write a letter of application following the format above and guidelines below.

> # Computer Tutor–Assistant Required
> Knowledge of word processing, presentation, and internet required.
> Must be able to show initiative and work as part of a team.
>
> Apply in writing to: Manager, Computer World, Co. Wicklow

Steps to be taken when applying for a job:
Step 1 read the advertisement and read it again
Step 2 underline/highlight the skills, qualities, experience required
Step 3 apply for the job using the method required in the advert, in this case by letter.

Draft your letter in the space over.

Electronic mail

E-mail is becoming a more and more popular way of applying for a job. To send an e-mail you must have a computer with internet access and specialist software packages which facilitate the delivery and receipt of e-mail, such as Eircom, Yahoo or Outlook Express. You also need to know the e-mail address of the person you want to send the mail to, e.g. sean@someplace.ie.

E-mail is

- **fast**
- **efficient**
- **cost-effective**

Get your Link Modules and computer teachers' e-mail addresses and send them an e-mail applying for the following job:

> # Busy play centre requires team leaders for Saturday and Sunday work.
>
> The successful candidate will be able to motivate, delegate and lead by example.
>
> Applications by e-mail to: *(Get your teacher's e-mail address)*

Telephone

We are all very familiar with telephones; we use them to contact people every day. However applying for a job by telephone requires preparation.

BEFORE THE CALL	DURING THE CALL	AFTER THE CALL
• Prepare what you are going to say. • Practice with a friend. • Make sure to have a pen and paper ready to take notes during the call.	• If you do not know the person's name, ask whom you are talking to. • Be very clear and speak slowly. • Put interest and expression into your voice. • Keep to the point. • Listen carefully to the speaker. • Take down any relevant information. • Thank the person for their time and attention.	• Re-read your notes and make sure you are clear on what was said.

ANSWER MACHINES

Leave a short (pre-rehearsed) message with the following information:
- your name
- your number
- say you will call back

Ireland's leading sales and merchandising agency requires a number of people to work calling on retail stores in your area to sell food products.

You will be expected to work to targets and achieve results in a very professional manner. You must have the ability to confidently communicate to retailers on a broad range of issues.

This is an ideal and exciting opportunity for anyone who would like to focus their career towards Sales and Business Development.

Apply by telephone to:
Sales Manager, telephone 145 8956

Role-play an application for the above position by telephone. Tape-record this activity to help you evaluate the experience.

Application forms
Job application forms can be lengthy, thought-provoking documents. The following guidelines should always be adhered to when completing an application form.

Guidelines
- Read the instructions carefully.
- Have your CV ready for reference.
- Photocopy the form so you can practice.
- Begin with simple questions.
- Jot down ideas for more difficult questions – work and rework these ideas.
- Fill in all the spaces.
- Proofread for spelling and grammar.
- Get a friend to double-check it.
- Fill in the actual form.
- Use clear block writing.

- Use a black pen.
- Do not use correction fluid.
- Keep the form in excellent condition.
- Keep a copy of the form as reference for when you're called for an interview.

Read the following extract from an application form. Note any errors you can find.

APPLICATION FORM

Please complete in block capitals

Personal Details

Title: Mr   First Name: John   Surname: Leary

Address: 20 Sweeney Lane, Malahide, Co. Dublin

Contact Number: (01) 833 3456

E-Mail Address: ~~john@yahoo.com~~ leary@home.ie

Secondary Education

Name of school: Howth Community   From: To:

Junior Cert. English B, Irish A, Maths C, French A,

Business A, Science C, Art B, CSPE A.

ERRORS

1	
2	
3	
4	

Application Form
Please complete in block capitals

Personal Details

Title: First name: Surname:

Address:

Telephone number:

E-mail:

Secondary Education

Name of school:

From   To

Qualifications

Qualification   Date taken

Junior Certificate

Subject	Level	Grade

Subject | Level | Grade

Leaving Certificate Vocational Programme

Date to be taken

Subject | Level | Grade

Work experience

1   Name of employer   Dates

Job title

Duties/responsibilities

What benefits have you gained from your work experience?

2   Name of employer   Dates

Job title

Duties/responsibilities

What benefits have you gained from your work experience?

3   Name of employer   Dates

Job title

Duties/responsibilities

What benefits have you gained from your work experience?

Any other qualifications/training

Detail any achievements (include dates received):

Detail your interests/hobbies and your level of participation:

What personal qualities/skills will you bring with you:

I declare the information given is accurate and true:

Signed:

Date:

Personal evaluation

Which method would you prefer to use when applying for a job?

Why?

Which method was your least favourite?

Why?

Have you identified any job-seeking skills you need to improve on?

How could you do this?

Did you learn anything about yourself that you did not previously know?

Curriculum Vitae (CV)

A CV is a summary statement of your education, qualifications, skills and work experience. Most advertised jobs would require a CV. You won't get jobs without an interview and you won't get an interview without a CV.

Rules for preparing a CV

- A CV must be typed on no more than two pages. Write a rough draft and then use a word processing package to type your CV.
- Use bullet points throughout the CV.
- Use reverse chronological order: when listing education, work experience etc. put the most recent item first.
- Be positive: use positive ways to describe yourself and include your positive qualities.
- Highlight your skills in each area of your CV.
- Use accurate information; do not put down false information. If you really do not read books, don't state you enjoy reading just to fill space, you will get caught out.
- Avoid over-use of the word 'I'. I am . . ., I was . . ., I enjoy . . . Start with a verb, noun or adjective (Have an aptitude for . . ., Excellent communicator. . ., Self-motivated . . ., Team-player with ability to work alone . . ., Enterprising secondary-school student . . .).

Complete the CV below. Remember this can get your foot in the door for an interview.

Core portfolio item

CURRICULUM VITAE
(no more than 2 pages)

Personal statement
Summary of your skills and qualities. It gives the employer a picture of you. Bullet points may be used.

_____

_____

_____

_____

Personal details
Include at least four pieces of personal information.

Name: _____

Address: _____

E-mail: _____

Telephone number: _____

Date of Birth: Day/Month/Year _____
You must use full digits, e.g. 04/07/1990

Education
Schools attended in reverse order (put the most recent first). Exams taken (include actual results) and those to be taken (include realistic predicted results). Include educational achievements.

Secondary education

Current school name and address: _____

Dates attending: _____

Leaving Certificate Vocational Programme (year)

SUBJECT	LEVEL	PREDICTED RESULT
Link modules	Common	

Transition year (optional)

Achievements

Junior certificate (year)

SUBJECT	LEVEL	RESULT

SUBJECT	LEVEL	RESULT

Primary education

School name and address:

Dates attended:

Work experience
Put down the most recent first. Include voluntary work.

Dates of work experience:

Employer's name and address:

Job title:

Duties and responsibilities:

Dates of work experience:

Employer's name and address:

Job title:

Duties and responsibilities:

Interests and hobbies

Include any of your interests and hobbies and your level of participation in each.

Achievements

Descriptions of your major achievements. These should back up your Personal profile above – they are the evidence that you can do what you say.

References

People who are willing to recommend you (usually one from your education, one from work experience). Not a relation.

Name: Name:

Title: Title:

Address: _____ Address: _____

Contact Number: _____ Contact Number: _____

This curriculum vitae can be submitted as a portfolio item so long as it does not link with any other portfolio item.

> **IT:** Use a word processing software package (e.g. Microsoft Word) to type up your curriculum vitae. It should be typed in Times New Roman font, size 12. Make headings and subheadings stand out by using **bold** and *italics*. It's a good idea to use tables or tabs when listing subjects and work experience details.

Job interviews

A successful interview is a two-way process. The interviewer finds out whether you match their requirements; you get the chance to assess the organisation – are they offering what you want? Interviews are all about proper preparation.

BEFORE THE INTERVIEW

- Identify and memorise your best selling points.
- Rehearse the key points you want to get across.
- Run through what you would say in the interview with a friend or colleague. If possible, tape or video yourself.
- Practice, practice, practice!
- Know the location of the interview and have a plan ready to get there on time.

DAY OF THE INTERVIEW

- An interview is formal: dress for the part.
- Arrive ten minutes early.
- Be polite to everyone you meet.

DURING THE INTERVIEW

- Adopt an open, relaxed posture.
- Make eye contact with the interviewer.
- Listen carefully and affirm questions with interviewer.
- Use appropriate body language.
- Speak clearly and confidently using normal conversational voice.
- Express ideas, opinions and points in a logical sequence.
- Take care not to drop voice at the end of sentences.

DURING THE INTERVIEW (Cont'd)

- Avoid reading from notes.
- Avoid distracting mannerisms, jargon, slang.
- Explain technical terms which may be unfamiliar to interviewer.
- Use action words and phrases when describing events (e.g. I planned ..., we evaluated ...).
- Make reference to skills gained through Link Module activities.

Students may include a video recording as an optional portfolio item. This option provides you with the opportunity to demonstrate your verbal communication skills. It can serve as a valuable preparation for future job interviews.

Optional portfolio item

RECORDED INTERVIEW
(3–5 minutes)
- Read the following advertisement.
- Prepare the questions below.
- Arrange for this interview to be recorded (video) so that this can be included in your portfolio.

COMPUTER TUTOR – ASSISTANT REQUIRED
Knowledge of word processing, presentation, and internet required.
Must be able to show initiative and work as part of a team.

Apply in writing to:
Manager, Computer World, Arklow, Co. Wicklow

Questions
Introductory information
- Tell me about yourself.
- How do you think a friend, colleague or employer would describe you?
- What are your greatest strengths and weaknesses?
- What are your hobbies and interests?

Education and work experience
- What are your LCVP subjects?
- What is your favourite LCVP subject? Why?
- What have you learned from your previous work experiences?
- What can you offer us?
- Why should we hire you for this position?
- Give me an example of when you had to deal with conflict in the workplace.

Organisational knowledge
- What do you know about this organisation?
- What types of work environment do you like best?

Career goals and aspirations
- What are your career goals and aspirations?
- How do you plan to achieve these goals?
- Where do you see yourself in five years or ten years from now?

Situational questions
- Give me an example of a time when you have shown initiative.
- Have you ever worked as part of a team? Give an example.

This recorded interview can be submitted as a portfolio item.

> **Note:**
> As a rule, references to an activity already reported or diaried by a student in his/her portfolio should not occupy more than twenty-five per cent of the recorded interview, i.e. two out of eight questions.

Exam questions

Q1.
Describe **four** steps you would take to prepare for a job interview.

_____

_____

_____

_____

_____

_____

_____

(8 marks)

Q2.

> # POSITION AVAILABLE
> for an <u>innovative</u> person
> to work in the **Business Development Division**
> of a medium-sized engineering firm
>
> Applicants must hold the <u>*ECDL*</u> or another <u>*IT*</u> qualification
> Apply with CV to:
> Personnel Manager
> EngTippCo
> Business Park
> Tipperary Town
> *EngTippCo is an <u>equal opportunities</u> employer*

(a) Explain **three** of the underlined words/terms.

_____

_____

_____

_____

_____

(6 marks)

(b) Outline **three** methods an employer may use to recruit employees.

_____

_____

_____

(6 marks)

Q3.

Wanted: part-time receptionist. Must have experience, good telephone manner and basic keyboard skills. Apply to: MRD Ltd, Main Street, Enniscorthy, Co. Wexford for an application form.

(a) Describe **two** qualities that would give you an advantage if you were applying for the above position.

(4 marks)

(b) Suggest **two** places where this advertisement should be placed to attract applicants and give **one** reason for choosing **each** of them.

(6 marks)

(c) Identify **three** steps that you should take to prepare for an interview for the above position.

(6 marks)

(d) Write a letter applying for the position of part-time receptionist as advertised.

(9 marks)

Q4.

Wanted: Enterprising person to join a stock control team.
Computer and keyboarding skills essential.
Apply with a Curriculum Vitae, listing two referees, to:
The Personnel Manager, Goblet Ltd, Ocean View, Killybegs, Co. Donegal.

(a) Name **two** advertising media where the above advertisement could be placed. Give **one** reason for each of the media you have named.

(4 marks)

(b) Why are applicants asked to list referees on their Curriculum Vitae?

(4 marks)

(c) Why do you think Goblet Ltd want an enterprising person?

(5 marks)

UNIT EVALUATION

Did you cover specific learning outcomes?

SPECIFIC LEARNING OUTCOME	COVERED (TICK)
2.1 recognise the different ways in which job vacancies are advertised 2.2 apply for a job by letter, telephone and e-mail 2.3 complete an application form 2.4 compile and create a curriculum vitae in word processed format 2.5 explain how to prepare for a job interview 2.6 engage in a simulated job interview	

Does this unit and your learning experience link with any other Leaving Certificate subjects?

SUBJECT	HOW IT LINKS

What was your favourite part of this unit and why?

_____

_____

_____

_____

_____

| Unit 3 | Career investigation |

This unit introduces the skills of career research and planning. Students should be encouraged and facilitated to actively investigate careers related to their aptitudes, interests and choice of Leaving Certificate subjects, with particular reference to their selected vocational subjects.

SPECIFIC LEARNING OUTCOMES

The student should be able to

3.1	identify personal aptitudes and interests	pp. 70–72
3.2	investigate a range of careers appropriate to personal aptitudes and interests	p. 74
3.3	identify and analyse the aptitudes and skills required to pursue a specific career	p. 87
3.4	describe relevant qualifications and training required for entry to the selected career	pp. 76–80
3.5	identify available opportunities to pursue a selected career locally, nationally, and where possible, at international level	pp. 80–81
3.6	plan and set up an opportunity to interview and/or work-shadow a person in a selected career	pp. 81–86
3.7	integrate information from a variety of sources to prepare a final report on a career investigation	pp. 87–92
3.8	reflect on and evaluate the experience of undertaking a career investigation	pp. 91–92
3.9	link the activities in this unit to learning in relevant Leaving Certificate subjects.	p. 96

EXPLORING YOU!

Most of us have had lots of ideas, as we have grown up, about what we would like to do with our lives. These ideas were probably formed because we wanted to be like someone we admired. Your choices may have led you in many different directions and thus you may feel confused about what one thing you want to do.

How do you know which direction you should take?

This unit should help you explore your aptitudes, interests and LCVP subjects and make it easier for you to develop career goals.

Aptitudes

What are aptitudes?

Aptitudes are natural talents, special abilities for doing, or learning to do, certain kinds of things.

Your aptitudes can help you decide on a possible career. Every occupation, whether it is engineering, medicine, mechanic or teaching, uses certain aptitudes. The work you are most likely to enjoy and be successful in is work that uses your aptitudes. If you lack the aptitudes required for a career, you may find the work difficult or unpleasant.

Identify your aptitudes

- **Do a recommended aptitude test, which is a way of evaluating how you perform on tasks or react to different situations.**
- **Talk to your career guidance teacher who will explore your results with you and help you identify careers based on these results.**

Where do your aptitudes lie?

List three talents that you have; areas you are really good in.

Examples: Musical ability, skill with numbers, design skills, verbal skills

Identify the careers that relate to your aptitudes

APTITUDE	POSSIBLE CAREER
Example:	
Skill with numbers	*Accountant or bank official*

Interests
(You identified your interests when preparing your CV)

What are interests?
Interests are activities that you usually don't have to force yourself to do and that make you feel good about yourself while you are doing them.

You can probably think of lots of things that fit this description. You might really enjoy watching television or socialising with friends, but these are not interests; interests are active pursuits that involve you doing, creating, or learning about something.

The better you understand your interests the better you will be able to analyse the relationship between your interests and your future career. The closer the match between interests and career choice, the more satisfying your work.

Identify your interests
Physical activities
Football, hurling, basketball, swimming, walking, yoga etc.

Creative activities
Art and craft, technical drawing, model-building etc.

Others

LCVP subjects

List your LCVP subjects below:

Link modules

Have you any favourite subjects?

Can you identify any career that may link with your favourite subjects?
Accounting and business: accountant, insurance official, entrepreneur, stockbroker, bank official.
Art and Music: musician, artist, designer, interior designer.

SUBJECT	CAREER

Identify your vocational subject groupings:
You chose two subjects that permitted you to qualify for LCVP.

Can you identify any career that may link with your vocational subject groupings?
Example: *Home Economics and Biology: you may wish to enter health care*
         Art and Business: you may wish to enter advertising
         Agricultural Science and Chemistry: you may wish to enter agri-business

Summary
Summarise aptitudes, interests and LCVP subjects required to pursue a career:

My personal profile

ABOUT ME	POSSIBLE CAREER OPTIONS
Results of aptitude test:	
My interests:	
My LCVP subjects: List in order of preference • • • • • • • •	
My vocational subject groupings: • •	

You have now identified a wide range of careers based on your aptitudes, interests and LCVP subjects. You now need to identify a specific career to investigate further.
Is there one area that you would now like to expolre?

I WOULD LIKE TO INVESTIGATE A CAREER IN:

Personal evaluation
Did you identify any personal interests or aptitudes that you did not realise you had?

Did any career appear in your personal profile that you had not considered before?

Is there any area in your personal profile that you could broaden or expand on?

How?

Qualifications and training

Investigate qualifications and training required for entry into your selected career. Identify how you can gain entry into your chosen career under as many of the options given below as possible:

Option 1

Name a *third level college*:

Course title:

Entry requirements:
Subjects and/or last year's points

Course duration:

Content of the course:

Qualification attained from this course:

Further training required to get into career *(optional)*:

Option 2
Name a *further education college*:

Course title:

Entry requirements:
Subjects/portfolio/interview

Course duration:

Content of the course:

Qualification attained from this course:

Further training required to get into career *(optional)*:

Option 3

Name a *private college*:

Course title:

Entry requirements:
Subjects/portfolio/interview

Fees:

Course duration:

Content of the course:

Qualification attained from this course:

Further training required to get into career *(optional)*:

Option 4
FÁS or Fáilte Ireland courses
How to apply:

Course title:

Entry requirements:
Subjects/interview

Course duration:

Content of the course:

Qualification attained from this course:

Further training required to get into career *(optional)*:

Option 5
On-the-job training
How to find a placement:
Answer an advertisement/networking/internet/recruitment fair/apply to targeted businesses/etc.

Duration of training:

What the training involves:

Qualification attained from this training:

Further training required to get into career *(optional)*:

Option 6
Study abroad
Name a college:

Course title:

Entry requirements:
Subjects/portfolio/interview

Fees:

Course duration:

Content of the course:

Qualification attained from this course:

Further training required to get into career *(optional)*:

Career opportunities
Identify future opportunities for you to pursue the career you have chosen under each of the following headings:

Locally
Can you identify any local business/voluntary group that you could work for once you have completed training for your chosen career?

Get help from:
local newspapers
local phone directories
class discussion
local business association

Example:

You want to be a hotel manager, you have completed a course in hotel management and now you would like some experience of working in this environment. Is there a local hotel you could work in?

_____

_____

_____

_____

Nationally

Can you identify any opportunities on a national level (somewhere in Ireland) that you could work for once you have completed training for your chosen career?

> **Get help from:**
> national newspapers
> golden pages
> internet
> recruitment agency
> class discussion

_____

_____

_____

Internationally

Can you identify any opportunities on an international level (somewhere outside Ireland) that you could work for once you have completed training for your chosen career?

> **Get help from:**
> internet
> class discussion
> somewhere you have seen on holidays
> foreign students / teachers in your school

_____

_____

_____

_____

Careers interview

Interviewing a person in your chosen career can give you a greater insight into this area. The following are guidelines to help you with this process.

If there is somebody else in your class interested in the same career area as you maybe you could work through this section as a pair. The advantages of working in a pair are:

- **You may feel less intimidated.**
- **Responsibility can be shared – one person could research a possible interviewee and the other could devise possible questions.**
- **Different roles can be assigned during the interview – one person could ask the questions and the other take notes.**

Steps in preparing for an interview:

Fill in the blank interview sheet below as you complete each step.

Step 1 Identify a person to be interviewed:
- **Ask someone you know.**
- **Have a class discussion, can any of your classmates help you out?**
- **See local phone directories and phone the business.**
- **Contact your local business association.**

Step 2 Phone the person to explain the purpose of the interview and organise an appropriate time for an interview:
- **Practice telephone techniques and what you need to say prior to calling (sometimes it may be good to write down or have a list of the items you need to say/ask).**
- **Bring your notes with you when making the call.**

Step 3 Draw up a questionnaire (see below):
- **Make sure all questions are relevant.**
- **Avoid any questions that may make your interviewee uncomfortable.**
- **Do not repeat questions.**
- **Read over the questions several times when you have completed the questionnaire. Make sure the questions make sense.**

Step 4 Interview recording method:
- **Are you going to take notes or will you ask the interviewee can you record the interview?**

Step 5 The interview
Make sure to thank the interviewee when the interview is complete and perhaps give them a small token to show your appreciation.

Career to be investigated:

_____

| **Career interview with:** |
| **Name of interviewee:** |
| **Place of employment:** |
| **Position:** |
| **Contact number:** |
| **Date:** |

Topic 1: Entry paths into the career
Qualification, subjects, cost of training, nature of training, minimum age, aptitudes etc.

Q. _____

A. _____

_____

_____

_____

Q. _____

A. _____

_____

_____

Topic 2: The workplace

On-job training, how workers are organised, products/services provided etc.

Q.

A.

Q.

A.

Q.

A.

Topic 3: Special skills and qualities needed
Personal/technical/interpersonal

Q.

A.

Q.

A.

Topic 4: Tasks and responsibilities
Description of typical day/week, people you meet, tasks carried out, areas of responsibility

Q.

A.

Q.

A.

Topic 5: Pay and conditions

Average salary, payment system, bonuses, holidays, trade union, health and safety

Q.

A.

Q.

A.

Q.

A.

> **Core portfolio item**

CAREER INVESTIGATION

(300–600 words)

Note: This can be typed or presented on an audio tape (3–5 minutes).

Description of duties involved in the career:

Identification of skills and qualities needed for this career:
Honest, reliable, hardworking, reality perception, good decision-maker etc.
Name each skill or quality and describe why it is required.

Identification of two different pathways to the career and qualifications and training needed for each:
Pick from two of the options you identified earlier in the unit.

Option 1
Name a course (place name and course title) you could take to help you in this career:

Entry requirements:

Content of this course:

Course duration:

Qualification attained from this course:

Option 2

Name a course (place name and course title) you could take to help you in this career:

Entry requirements:

Content of this course:

Course duration:

Qualification attained from this course:

Summary

What did you learn from the research into yourself and into career?

Aptitudes

What did you learn about yourself? (What type of aptitudes do you have?)

What did you learn about career? (Will those aptitudes help in your career?)

Interests

What did you learn about yourself? (Have you a lot/very few interests?)

What did you learn about career? (Do your interests link with your career choice?)

LCVP subjects

What did you learn about yourself? (Do you have favourite/best subjects?)

What did you learn about career? (Will these subjects help you at third level or in your career?)

Out-of-school activity
Interview, open day, work-shadowing

Details

What did you learn about yourself?

What did you learn about career?

The career

Do you still want to follow this career path?

Why/Why not?

Are there any new skills you will require for this career?

The career investigation

What did you get out of doing this investigation?

Do you have the correct LCVP subjects?

Will you be required to complete an entry interview for your course?

Have you developed any skills in completing this investigation?
Communication skills: conducting an interview; computer skills: typing investigation, research on the net

Sources of information
Include books, websites, magazines etc.

_____

_____

Signed: _____

Date: _____

This career investigation can be submitted as a portfolio item so long as it does not link with any other portfolio item.

> **IT: Use a word processing software package (e.g. Microsoft Word) to type up your career investigation. It should be typed in Times New Roman font, size 12. Make headings and subheadings stand out by using bold and *italics*.**

Exam questions

Q1.

You have been asked to complete a career investigation on a job of your choice. You must present your findings as a one-page poster. Set out your findings below giving at least **five** items of information.

(10 marks)

Q2.

Career choice is important so that you select a career that best suits your aptitudes and abilities.

(a) Name a career you have investigated.

Career:

(1 mark)

(b) List **three** qualities you have which makes this a suitable career for you.

_____

_____

_____

_____

_____

_____

(6 marks)

(c) Identify **two** of your Leaving Certificate subjects which you consider the most relevant for this career. Explain why each subject is relevant.

_____

_____

_____

_____

_____

_____

_____

(8 marks)

(d) Describe how you went about investigating the career mentioned.

_____

_____

_____

_____

_____

_____

_____

_____

_____

(10 marks)

(e) Evaluate the process of doing a career investigation:

_____

_____

_____

_____

_____

_____

UNIT EVALUATION

Did you cover specific learning outcomes?

SPECIFIC LEARNING OUTCOME	COVERED (TICK)
3.1 identify personal aptitudes and interests	
3.2 investigate a range of careers appropriate to personal aptitudes and interests	
3.3 identify and analyse the aptitudes and skills required to pursue a specific career	
3.4 describe relevant qualifications and training required for entry to the selected career	
3.5 identify available opportunities to pursue a selected career locally, nationally, and where possible, at international level	

SPECIFIC LEARNING OUTCOME	COVERED (TICK)
3.6 plan and set up an opportunity to interview and/or work-shadow a person in a selected career	
3.7 integrate information from a variety of sources to prepare a final report on a career investigation	
3.8 reflect on and evaluate the experience of undertaking a career investigation	
3.9 link the activities in this unit to learning in relevant Leaving Certificate subjects.	

Does this unit and your learning experience link with any other Leaving Certificate subjects?

SUBJECT	HOW IT LINKS

What was your favourite part of this unit and why?

Did you encounter any problems during this unit? How could you overcome these problems in future?

PROBLEM	SOLUTION

| Unit 4 | Work placement |

In this unit students are encouraged to plan, organise and engage in a work experience or work-shadowing placement. If possible, the placement should be consistent with students' career aspirations. This gives practical experience of the adult working environment as well as helping to develop the students' organisational and communicative skills. The unit should conclude with a de-briefing session where students are encouraged and facilitated to reflect on and evaluate their experiences.

SPECIFIC LEARNING OUTCOMES
The student should be able to

4.1	specify particular personal goals in relation to a work placement	p. 99
4.2	plan and organise a work placement	pp. 100–102
4.3	attend punctually for a specific placement	pp. 102–111
4.4	dress appropriately for a specific placement	pp. 102–111
4.5	follow a set of procedures in accordance with specific instructions	pp. 102–111
4.6	communicate effectively with other workers in a particular placement	pp. 102–111
4.7	follow a specific set of instructions relating to health and safety	pp. 102–111
4.8	review personal experiences in relation to a work placement	pp. 109–111
4.9	analyse reports by adults of personal performance in a workplace	p. 102
4.10	reflect on and evaluate a specific work placement in the light of career aspirations	p. 110
4.11	describe how what has been learned can be applied to work at home, in school and in the community	pp. 110–111
4.12	present a diary or written or verbal report on a specific work placement	pp. 103–111
4.13	link the activities in this unit to learning in relevant Leaving Certificate subjects.	p. 116

Work experience or work-shadowing?
Work experience is about engaging in a job, where as work-shadowing is about observing a job. Both are beneficial for you and are often regarded as one of the high points of the Leaving Certificate Vocational Programme.

What will you get from work experience/shadowing?

Job-seeking skills

- researching
- networking
- letter-writing
- application forms

- CVs
- making phone calls
- preparing for interviews
- presenting yourself

An understanding of working life

- travelling to and from work
- timekeeping and punctuality
- following instructions
- meeting deadlines

- relating to supervisors
- dealing with customers
- working as part of a team
- health and safety practice

First-hand knowledge of careers

- the type of work involved
- skills and qualities required
- ups and downs of the job
- related career areas
- useful contact people

Identify five personal goals that you want to get from this experience and state why.

PERSONAL GOAL	WHY?
1	
2	
3	
4	
5	

Planning a placement

What to do?

Ideally this placement will be organised with your career aspirations and interests in mind. In each of the following categories, can you identify a possible relevant placement?

CATEGORY	POSSIBLE PLACEMENT
Your interests:	
Your favourite Leaving Certificate subjects:	
Your aptitudes:	

What experiences and skills would you hope to get from a placement?

_____

_____

_____

_____

I would like to do my work experience or shadowing in the following area:

Where to go?

Having identified an area of interest you must now find a placement. Under each of the following headings locate a possible organisation to contact.

	NAME OF ORGANISATION	CONTACT NAME	CONTACT NUMBER/ ADDRESS
Local area			
Local paper/ shop windows			
Family/friend			
Internet			
School database of previous placements			

Write (see page 45) or telephone (see page 49) all the organisations you are interested in doing a placement with.

When you get responses select the placement you are most interested in. Thank all the others for their time and for considering you for work experience or shadowing in their organisation.

Checklist for work experience/shadowing

Before the placement

- Organise a placement relevant to your career aspirations and interests.
- Fill in all relevant paperwork and get it to the relevant people before the deadlines given.
- Be sure you are aware of the information you need to get while on the placement.
- Get a copy of an evaluation sheet that the employer should complete about your performance in the placement.
- Ring the placement the day before to confirm starting times etc.
- Make sure you are very clear about the location of the placement and how to get there.

During the placement

- Fill in your diary each day.
- Attend each day punctually – if there is a problem and you cannot attend one day ring both the employer and your school.
- Dress appropriately for the placement.
- Follow all the instructions and procedures given to you.
- Communicate effectively with all workers.
- Follow all health and safety instructions.
- Ask as many questions as you can to give you more information about this career.
- On the last day ask your employer to fill in an evaluation sheet and to return it to your school (you could take it back with you if it is completed on time).

After the placement

- Review your personal experiences in relation to the placement.
- Analyse the report completed by your employer on your personal performance.
- Write a letter thanking the employer and their staff for allowing you to do your work placement with them.

Optional portfolio item

WORK EXPERIENCE/SHADOWING DIARY
(1000–1500 words)
Note: Three entries are required for this diary.

Introductory page

Student name:

Name of employer:

Address of employer:

Name of person you are shadowing:
(For work-shadowing only)

Title of job:

Brief description of job:

Why I selected this area:

Future career/career investigation:

Interests:

Aptitudes:

LCVP Subjects:

Research and paperwork (Diary entry 1)

Date:

Time started:

Research into area for work-shadowing:
Examples: Internet, golden pages, phone calls, school database, local business, local newspapers etc.

Method 1

Information obtained:

What did I learn from this?

Method 2

Information obtained:

What did I learn from this?

Paperwork completed

Were you required to complete paperwork by your school or employer in order to obtain your placement? Were there deadlines for this paperwork? If so give details.

What did I learn from this?

Work-shadowing (Diary entry 2)

Date:

Time started:

Time finished:

Main observations:

Work observed today:

What did I learn:

What did I feel:

Work observed today:

What did I learn:

What did I feel:

Problems encountered/challenges faced and how you overcame them:

Interaction with staff and how you found this:
What perception did they have of you?

Work-shadowing (Diary entry 3)

Date:

Time started:

Time finished:

Main observations:

Work observed today:

What did I learn:

What did I feel:

Work observed today:

What did I learn:

What did I feel:

Problems encountered/challenges faced and how you overcame them:

Interaction with staff and how you found this:
What perception did they have of you?

Evaluation (Diary entry 4)

Date:

Time:

Did you enjoy this experience?

Do you feel you are suited to this particular organisation and working environment?

Evaluation of experience in light of career aspirations:
Are you still interested in this career? Why/why not?

Skills and experience acquired or improved:

How can I apply what I learned?
At home
Do you now appreciate what a working day involves (understand what your parents have to do each day)? Could you help out with something at home from skills you developed?

At school

Will you study harder? Are you now more organised? Do you realise the importance of time management?

In my local community

Could you now use the skills you developed/observed to aid your community (voluntary work)?

Appendices

Up to two items may be included. Examples might include a form used for personal debriefing or an evaluation completed by the student's supervisor, which students should analyse for personal reference.

This work-shadowing diary can be submitted as a portfolio item so long as it does not link with any other portfolio item.

> **IT: Use a word processing software package (e.g. Microsoft Word) to type up your diary. It should be typed in Times New Roman font, size 12. Make headings and subheadings stand out by using bold and *italics*.**

Exam questions

Q1.

You have returned to school after your work experience or work-shadowing. Your teacher has asked you to review how you got on and has spent some time on feedback.

(a)   Give **two** criteria you would use to assess how successful your work experience was.

(4 marks)

(b)   Why is feedback important?

(4 marks)

(c)   Communicating with other workers is one criterion your employer will evaluate you on.

   (i)   Why is this criterion considered important?

(6 marks)

(ii) If you received an unsatisfactory report in this area, what steps could you take to improve your communication skills?

_____

_____

_____

(3 marks)

(iii) Identify and explain **four** ways you observed health and safety regulations being implemented in the workplace where you did your work experience or work-shadowing.

_____

_____

_____

_____

_____

_____

_____

(8 marks)

Q2.

You are required to write a letter of thanks to your employer after you return from work experience. Your letter should include reference to how you benefited from the work experience and how it will help you in the future.

_____

_____

_____

(10 marks)

Q3.
You are required to find work experience/shadowing as part of the LCVP programme.
(a)   List **three** ways of finding work experience/shadowing.

(3 marks)

(b) Mention **two** advantages of any one of the ways you have listed above.

(4 marks)

(c) State **three** benefits of participating in work experience.

(3 marks)

(d) On completing work experience you are required to write a report showing what you have learned. Outline **five** items to be included in this report.

(15 marks)

UNIT EVALUATION

Did you cover specific learning outcomes?

SPECIFIC LEARNING OUTCOME	COVERED (TICK)
4.1 specify particular personal goals in relation to a work placement	
4.2 plan and organise a work placement	
4.3 attend punctually for a specific placement	
4.4 dress appropriately for a specific placement	
4.5 follow a set of procedures in accordance with specific instructions	
4.6 communicate effectively with other workers in a particular placement	
4.7 follow a specific set of instructions relating to health and safety	
4.8 review personal experiences in relation to a work placement	
4.9 analyse reports by adults of personal performance in a workplace	
4.10 reflect on and evaluate a specific work placement in the light of career aspirations	
4.11 describe how what has been learned can be applied to work at home, in school and in the community	
4.12 present a diary or written or verbal report on a specific work placement	
4.13 link the activities in this unit to learning in relevant Leaving Certificate subjects.	

Does this unit and your learning experience link with any other Leaving Certificate subjects?

SUBJECT	HOW IT LINKS

What was your favourite part of this unit and why?

Did you encounter any problems during this unit? How could you overcome these problems in future?

PROBLEM	SOLUTION

Unit 4 – Work placement

Link Module 2
Enterprise Education

| Unit 5 | Enterprise skills |

The purpose of this unit is to introduce students to the skills of enterprise and entrepreneurship such as idea-generation, risk-assessment, problem-solving, teamwork, leadership and commitment. The learning outcomes can be achieved through a combination of classroom teaching, participation in a variety of skill-building exercises and interaction with enterprising adults from business and the community.

SPECIFIC LEARNING OUTCOMES
The student should be able to

5.1	describe the qualities and skills of enterprising people	pp. 120–124
5.2	recognise examples of personal, community and entrepreneurial enterprise	pp. 124–127, 132–133
5.3	identify personal strengths and weaknesses	p. 127
5.4	suggest a course of action appropriate to improving personal enterprise skills	p. 128
5.5	work co-operatively with others as part of a team	pp. 129–130
5.6	appreciate the value of teamwork in generating ideas, assessing risks, solving problems and completing tasks	pp. 130–131
5.7	undertake leadership of a group in an appropriate activity	p. 129
5.8	plan and organise a meeting	pp. 134–137
5.9	make a presentation to peers and to adults	p. 144
5.10	link the activities in this unit to learning in relevant Leaving Certificate subjects	p. 151
5.11	evaluate the successes achieved and problems encountered in this unit.	pp. 151–152

WHAT IS ENTERPRISE?
Enterprise is a culture affecting all aspects of our lives. Enterprise is all around us in our personal lives, in our communities and entrepreneurial activities. Enterprise is about showing initiative and taking risks. This unit describes how we can be enterprising and how enterprise is all around us.

Qualities and skills of enterprising people
Students, workers, community activists, voluntary workers and those who establish organisations are all enterprising people. Enterprising people have certain qualities that allow them to perform as they do. They also develop skills which complement these qualities.

Read the following statements about enterprising people. Then decide if you agree, are not sure or disagree with each statement.

STATEMENT	AGREE	NOT SURE	DISAGREE
An enterprising person is:			
Only interested in making money			
Was born, not made that way			
Wants to make jobs for people			
Is well educated			
Doesn't like making decisions			
Is prepared to take risks			
Understands and gets on with people			
Can communicate well			
Is realistic			
Always comes up with an original idea			

As a class, discuss your decisions. Decide on a class definition of what an enterprising person is (you can put several of these statements together or come up with your own). An enterprising person is:

_____

_____

_____

_____

_____

_____

Now identify skills and qualities of the enterprising person you have defined.
Here are some examples of the skills and qualities you would expect to find in an
enterprising person. Can you think why each of these has been selected?

SKILLS AND QUALITIES	REASON FOR SELECTION
Determined	They really want their idea/project to work and will put all their effort and resources into seeing it through.
Realistic	
Creative	
Risk-taker	
Self-confident	
Good decision-maker	
Adaptable	

Can you think of some of your own?

SKILL/QUALITY	REASON FOR SELECTION

Read the following case study and identify enterprising qualities and skills in Claire. Back each quality up with relevant material from the case study.

Case study

Claire is a fifth-year LCVP student. She and her classmates are about to take part in an enterprise activity. Claire is looking forward to this as she really enjoyed planning and taking part in the numerous transition-year activities the previous year. She knew this activity would be a success. The class held a meeting to discuss ideas; Claire listened carefully to everybody's ideas and then made her suggestion. Claire thought a table quiz for first-year students would be good. She felt it would help the first-year students to get to know each other in a social setting and they could raise money for charity by charging an admission on each table. Everybody liked Claire's idea and voted in favour of it. Claire was elected group leader.

SKILL/QUALITY	REASON FOR SELECTION

Are you enterprising?

Look at each of the following areas of your life. Make a note on how you feel you are enterprising in each one.

WHERE AM I ENTERPRISING?

At Home *Do you make the dinner without being asked – showing initiative? Do you decide not to persist in asking your parents for something they have already denied you – being realistic? Do you baby-sit younger siblings?*

In sport *Are you a team player? Are you a team captain? Do you show initiative? Are you a reliable member of the team?*

Hobbies *Are you part of any non-sporting groups where you are a team player and come up with ideas? Are you creative?*

At school/study *Do you get homework and assignments in on time – time management? Do you take part in extra-curricular activities, e.g. green schools committee, school magazine, debating? Have you organised any activities in school? Are you a prefect or a mentor for younger students?*

Part time/holiday work *Can you think of a time when you had to show initiative, be decisive, work as part of a team?*

Other

Evaluation of exercise

Do you think you are enterprising?

Are there any areas in your life in which you are very enterprising?

Are there any areas in your life in which you could be more enterprising?

How could you do this?

SWOT

SWOT analysis is used to analyse what you are doing now and to help in identifying your future.

SWOT stands for:

S: Strengths – these are internal to us, we have them now.

W: Weaknesses – these are internal to us, we have them now.

Strengths and weaknesses are internal. We affect them and can change them.

O: Opportunities – these are external and are in the future.

T: Threats – these are external and are in the future.

Opportunities and threats are external. They are affected by external factors and therefore are more difficult for us to control.

SWOT and you

Complete this SWOT analysis of yourself.

STRENGTHS	WEAKNESSES
What are your strengths? **What are you good at?** *Example: self-confidence*	**List your weaknesses** **– areas of your life you could improve.** *Example: French*
OPPORTUNITIES	THREATS
What opportunities lie ahead **of you in the future?** *Example: travel*	**Can you see anything that could** **threaten the future you want?** *Example: lack of employment in your local area*

Eliminating your weaknesses

A weakness is internal, you can change it. How can you turn your weaknesses into strengths? Examine each weakness identified above and identify steps you could take to turn this weakness into a strength.

Example: French

- **Make a study plan for French.**
- **Go to an extra French class or ask for extra French homework.**
- **Work very hard.**
- **Try to organise a French exchange or go to a French summer camp.**

WEAKNESS	STEPS TO TAKE TO IMPROVE

Eliminating threats

Threats are affected by external factors and are harder to change. However you can try to turn the threat into an opportunity.

Example: Lack of employment in your local area.

- *Opportunity: you could travel, work abroad.*

Can you turn any of your threats into opportunities?

THREAT	OPPORTUNITY

What is teamwork?

Teamwork means working as part of a group in which there is a shared goal. Teamwork is the ability to put aside personal goals and work together for a common purpose. In the past when we thought of teams we thought of sport, however the concept has spread from the world of sports to business. Teamwork is a very important element of LCVP.

The benefit of teams

Teams achieve results that would not be possible if people were to work alone.

- **A great variety of skills and experiences is available.**
- **Decisions are supported and made together.**
- **A team is constantly learning and improving itself.**
- **Diversity of opinions and ideas is encouraged.**
- **A sense of belonging and pride in accomplishments develops.**
- **Problems can be shared and solved as a group.**
- **Work can be completed much faster than if the task were to be done alone.**

Team-building

Team-building is about encouraging a group of people to work together. There are five stages in team-building:

1. *Forming:* **a group of people comes together for the first time. Roles and responsibilities are distributed at this stage.**
2. *Storming:* **it is normal for differences of opinion to arise (different goals, roles etc.) when a team has been formed. The process of solving such conflicts is storming.**
3. *Norming:* **team members know each other well. The team is in agreement on how they should behave and how the group should progress.**
4. *Performing:* **things are starting to work and results are being achieved.**
5. *Transforming/Mourning:* **once the team completes its project, the group takes on a new role or is disbanded. There can be sense of loss as the project winds up and this is why this stage is referred to as mourning.**

Leadership

The team leader is the person responsible for ensuring the objective is fulfilled. They co-ordinate the group's activities. Over the two years of completing Link Modules each person in your class should be given the opportunity to lead a group.

A leader should be
- **fair**
- **supportive**
- **a good delegate**
- **a good communicator**
- **organised**
- **have the ability to make final decisions**

Team activity

As a class organise yourselves around the classroom in order of age, starting with the oldest person.

Stage 1: Forming

Appoint a team leader to co-ordinate the task.

Stage 2: Storming

Make sure everyone is clear on who the leader is and how the task will be carried out. Solve any disputes that may arise.

Stage 3: Norming

Clarify issues on how the tasks will be completed with all group members. The team should be in complete agreement.

Stage 4: Performing

Begin to organise yourselves into age order starting with the oldest group member.

Stage 5: Transforming/Mourning

The task is complete. Group members can sit back down.

Evaluation:

1. Discuss this activity as a class to evaluate your teamwork skills.
2. Answer the following questions (alone) on the activity:

Would you prefer to be a team leader or a team player?

Did some members of the group work harder than others?

Was the team leader effective?

Did your group have any conflicts and how were these conflicts solved?

Did this activity take a long time? What factors affected the time taken? Did you complete the activity? If not, why not?

Community enterprise

Entrepreneurial activity in a community does not just involve money-making by individuals. People often get together to use their enterprise skills and talents, on a voluntary basis, to help others or improve their community. For example, many towns have a Tidy Towns committee, a St Vincent de Paul Society, youth clubs, residents' associations etc.

Unit 6 deals with this in more detail.

Identify organisations in your community under each of the following areas:

AREA	ORGANISATION NAME
Sport and recreation	
Youth	
Community welfare	
Environment	

Discuss your findings with your class to compile a large directory of local community enterprises.

Entrepreneurial enterprise

What is an entrepreneur?

Entrepreneurs are people who have the ability to spot and evaluate business opportunities, to gather the necessary resources to take advantage of them and to take appropriate action and risks to ensure success.

Entrepreneurs are action-oriented, highly motivated individuals who take calculated risks to achieve goals. Without entrepreneurs in an economy little business development or wealth creation would occur. Unit 6 deals with this in more detail.

What is an intrapreneur?

The intrapreneur differs from the entrepreneur, as they do not take the financial risk in starting up the business venture. An intrapreneur is somebody who works within an organisation and shows entrepreneurial qualities and skills.

Identify entrepreneurs in your area under the following headings:

AREA	ENTERPRISE NAME
Farming/Fishing/Forestry/Mining	
Construction/Manufacturing	
Retailers/Wholesalers	
Financial institutions	
Tourism	
Other	

Discuss your findings with your class to compile a large directory of local entrepreneurial enterprises.

Meetings

A meeting is a formal gathering of people, gathering for a common purpose. Unless properly planned and executed, meetings can be a terrible waste of time. Every meeting should have a chairperson and a secretary.

Functions of a chairperson

- Determine the agenda for the meeting and make sure this agenda is adhered to.
- Ensure that everything operates in an efficient manner and in accordance with any previously agreed rules.
- Give everyone the opportunity to speak.
- Oversee any votes taken.
- Ensure the meeting starts and ends on time.
- Inform people that the meeting is taking place (when and where).

Functions of a secretary

- Book/organise a room if required.
- Deal with correspondence.
- Prepare the agenda for the meeting (in consultation with the chairperson).
- Send a copy of the agenda to those who require one.
- Take the minutes of the meeting.

Steps in organising a meeting

- Elect a chairperson and secretary.
- Draw up an agenda.
- Make sure everyone in the class has a copy of the agenda.

What is an agenda?

- It includes the date, time and venue for the meeting.
- It lists items to be discussed at the meeting.
- First item: minutes of the last meeting.
- Last item: Any Other Business (AOB), where people at the meeting are given the opportunity to discuss any items not included on the agenda.

What are minutes?

- A summary of the items discussed at the meeting.
- Each item on the agenda is included in the minutes.
- Minutes are taken by the secretary.

Team activity

Pick a high-profile enterprising person you would be interested in compiling a profile on. Team up with two or three others in your class interested in the same area.

Enterprise to explore:

Team members:

Have a meeting to delegate jobs in order to compile the profile. Draw up an agenda for this meeting:

AGENDA
Title:
Date:
Time:
Venue:
Chairperson:
Secretary:
Agenda
Minutes from last meeting

AOB (Any Other Business)

Signed: _____ (Secretary)

The secretary should take minutes at the meeting. Make sure to write down names of people who agree to do a job and when they agree to do it by.

MINUTES OF MEETING

Meeting topic:

Date:

Time:

Venue:

Chairperson:

Secretary:

Minutes on each item discussed

Signed: _____ **(Secretary)**

Compile a profile of the enterprising person.

Prepare a summary report on your findings.

Core portfolio item

SUMMARY REPORT
(300–600 words)

Prepared by:

Title of report:
What the report is about.

Terms of reference
Instructions given to the report writer.

Aims
Can be included in place of terms of reference. What you and your group want to get from the activity.
Group aims

Individual aims

Body of report

Divide the report into three or more sub-headings. There must be a logical sequence to summarise your main findings. You may decide to place paragraphs in order of importance, or in chronological order, depending on the subject matter of the summary report. The use of numbered or bold headings and bulleted lists is recommended.

Subheading 1

Subheading 2

Subheading 3

Conclusions

Must link with aims and report content.

Group conclusions

Individual conclusions

Recommendations

Suggestions for future action. Recommendations might also include ideas for follow-on activities or describe how you might perform better in a future exercise.

Signed:

This summary report can be submitted as a portfolio item so long as it does not link with any other portfolio item.

> **IT: Use a word processing software package (e.g. Microsoft Word) to type up your report. It should be typed in Times New Roman font, size 12. Make headings and subheadings stand out by using bold and *italics*.**

Read the notes below and use a presentation package (PowerPoint) or acetates to present your findings on the entrepreneur profiled to your teacher and classmates.

Presentations

Visual display
- Keep visual information to a minimum.
- Only include main points to be discussed.
- Do not overload with pictures or word art.

Oral communication
- Speak clearly.
- Do not rush information.
- Make eye contact with listeners.
- Use appropriate language so those listening can clearly understand you.
- Do not go over allocated time.
- Give your audience time to ask questions.

Optional portfolio item

PRESENTATION

(3–5 minutes)

A short presentation (supported by simple visual aids) given by the student, based on a specific enterprise activity in which he/she has participated, followed by two or three questions.

This recorded presentation can be submitted as a portfolio item so long as it does not link with any other portfolio item.

Evaluate the activity

Personal evaluation

What did you get from this activity? Did you learn information you did not previously know? Did you improve any skills?

Group evaluation

Have a discussion among group members. Did you work well together?

Class evaluation

The class should discuss in an orderly manner each group's investigation of the business they investigated.

Exam questions

Q1.

Teamwork occurs when a group of people work together towards a common goal.
(a) Identify **one** teamwork activity in which you have been involved.

(2 marks)

(b) Evaluate the teamwork element of the activity identified in (a) explaining, with examples, **three** aspects that worked well or did not work well. Give reasons for your answer.

(9 marks)

(c) Name **three** different sources of support or help available to you during the activity identified in (a). Explain in detail how **one** of the sources named above assisted you.

(5 marks)

(d) Why do many organisations emphasise the importance of teamwork? Include **three** reasons for your answer.

(9 marks)

Q2.

Sally Johnson was always interested in woodwork. For a number of years she helped out at a local furniture factory. With the help of the local enterprise board she carried out market research on the furniture industry. Her research showed that a potential market existed in the area of custom-made furniture. Using her savings and a loan from a bank she set up a small production enterprise to manufacture custom-built furniture. She now employs nine people organised into three teams, each team specialising in a different aspect of the making of the furniture. All furniture is made specially to order for each customer.

(a) Name **three** skills or qualities which Sally needed when setting up her business.

(6 marks)

(b)   Identify **two** benefits of working in teams.

(4 marks)

(c)   Describe **five** ways in which Sally could evaluate the success of her enterprise.

(15 marks)

Q3.

Mark has always had an interest in catering. When he left school he took a catering course and after working for five years in a large restaurant he decided to set up his own catering enterprise. He applied for and was granted a business unit in the local enterprise centre. He received a grant from the local enterprise board to help set up the enterprise. He prepared a business plan for the next three years and he also received approval for a loan from a local bank. He now employs six people, provides daily supplies to local shops and caters for private functions.

(a) Name **four** qualities Mark needed when setting up his own business.

(4 marks)

(b) Why do you think Mark was successful in receiving the grant and loan approval? Give **three** reasons for your answer.

(6 marks)

(c)   List **two** qualities Mark should look for when recruiting staff.

(4 marks)

(d)   Describe **four** ways in which Mark could evaluate the success of his enterprise.

(11 marks)

UNIT EVALUATION

Did you cover specific learning outcomes?

SPECIFIC LEARNING OUTCOME	COVERED (TICK)
5.1 describe the qualities and skills of enterprising people	
5.2 recognise examples of personal, community and entrepreneurial enterprise	
5.3 identify personal strengths and weaknesses	
5.4 suggest a course of action appropriate to improving personal enterprise skills	
5.5 work co-operatively with others as part of a team	
5.6 appreciate the value of teamwork in generating ideas, assessing risks, solving problems and completing tasks	
5.7 undertake leadership of a group in an appropriate activity	
5.8 plan and organise a meeting	
5.9 make a presentation to peers and to adults	
5.10 link the activities in this unit to learning in relevant Leaving Certificate subjects	
5.11 evaluate the successes achieved and problems encountered in this unit.	

Does this unit and your learning experience link with any other Leaving Certificate subjects?

SUBJECT	HOW IT LINKS

What was your favourite part of this unit, and why?

_____

_____

_____

_____

Did you encounter any problems during this unit? How could you overcome these problems in future?

PROBLEM	SOLUTION

| Unit 6 | **Local business enterprises** |

The purpose of this unit is to make students aware of what is involved in setting up and running an enterprise. Students should be encouraged to meet with entrepreneurs and investigate local business enterprises. Many of the learning outcomes of this unit may be achieved by students' engaging in a local study of 'My Own Place'. This unit should be integrated with Unit 1.

SPECIFIC LEARNING OUTCOMES
The student should be able to

6.1	identify a range of enterprises in the local community	p. 154
6.2	understand how an enterprise starts up and what support/training is available	pp. 154–157
6.3	describe the steps required to plan and carry out an investigation of a local enterprise	pp. 158–165
6.4	use learning from relevant Leaving Certificate subjects to formulate questions about aspects of a local enterprise	p. 164
6.5	organise a visit to a local enterprise and invite appropriate speakers to visit the group in school	pp. 167–170
6.6	carry out a SWOT analysis of a business	p. 166
6.7	report accurately on a visit by an entrepreneur to the classroom and on a class visit to a local enterprise	pp. 164, 170–175
6.8	compare and contrast information gathered on a group visit to a local enterprise	pp. 165–166
6.9	describe a local enterprise with particular reference to products, services, markets and workforce	p. 164
6.10	understand and describe the different roles of adults working in a business environment	p. 164
6.11	describe the impact of the Single European Market on a specific enterprise	p. 164
6.12	describe and evaluate the use of information and communicationtechnologies in a business enterprise	p. 164
6.13	understand the importance of education and training in the development of a business enterprise	p. 164
6.14	link the activities in this unit to learning in relevant Leaving Certificate subjects	p. 185
6.15	evaluate the successes achieved and problems encountered in this unit.	p. 185

Unit 6 – Local business enterprises

LOCAL BUSINESS ENTERPRISE

Every community is made up of a wide range of enterprises. In unit 5 (page 133) you identified entrepreneurs and business enterprise in your locality (if you have not covered this unit yet complete the worksheet now).

Benefits of business enterprise

Business enterprise benefits the local community by

- **creating employment; each business enterprise create jobs for people living in the local community**
- **increasing disposable income in the area; when people are working they have more money to spend on goods and services**
- **offering a wide range of products and services; each enterprise will offer a product or service that perhaps was not previously available to the community**
- **improving local people's skills and work experience; local people working in the business enterprise will develop skills they previously did not have and this will make them more employable**
- **encouraging further enterprise; when a business enterprise locates in an area it can often attract further enterprise.**

Business start-up and support

When starting up a business there are many common concerns that entrepreneurs have.

What business should I choose?

The entrepreneur's main aim is to make a profit. They must identify a niche (gap) in the market, take risks and exploit this gap.

What is a business plan and do I need one?

A business plan is very important; it helps the entrepreneur to focus. It sets clear goals which should help investors assess risk when investing in the business.

A business plan should be set out under the following headings:

1. **The business** (brief description of what is involved)
2. **The owners** (who owns the business)
3. **Management** (people responsible for day-to-day running of the business)
4. **The product**
5. **Marketing** (marketing mix see p.231)
6. **Production** (equipment required and units to be produced)
7. **Finance** (plan and sources of finance see p.156)
8. **Signature**

A business plan should not be mixed up with an enterprise plan.

Prepare a business plan for a group cake sale.
The plan is about the future. Write in the future tense.

Business plan

The business

The owners

Management

The product(s)

Marketing mix (see p.231)

Product

Price

Place

Promotion

Production

Finance

Signed:

Where can I find investors? (Sources of finance)

An entrepreneur can source capital from a bank in the form of a loan. Shareholders can buy shares in a company. The government offers grants for viable business ideas.

How will the Single European Market (SEM) impact my business?

Financial Assistance: the EU works with the Irish government and offers huge financial assistance to Irish business.

Barrier-free EU: this allows the free movement of trade. Irish companies can import and export goods from all over the EU.

Euro market: this eliminates the problems associated with exchange rates when importing and exporting.

Free movement of labour: EU citizens can work in any EU country without a work visa, so Irish businesses have a wide range of skilled employees available.

Survival: due to free trade there is huge competition for all EU enterprise and only the efficient enterprise will survive.

Read the following business profile and identify the impact SEM has had on the business.

Jones Timber Ltd is a medium-sized enterprise making wooden play equipment for children. Jones Timber Ltd has recently expanded and employed a further ten staff members thanks to an EU grant. Two of these new employees are skilled carpenters with unique skills from Spain.

Jones Timber Ltd imports some of their raw materials from France. They find trading much easier thanks to the euro.

Jones Timber Ltd now has a very user-friendly website and has noticed a huge increase in exports.

Jones Timber Ltd is a thriving, growing enterprise.

IMPACT OF SEM ON JONES TIMBER LTD	
Type of impact	Example from case study
1	
2	
3	
4	

What risks should I be aware of?
Entrepreneurs are risk-takers and take many different types of risk. They take financial risk, personal risk of failure, risk of competition etc.

Are some locations better than others?
Location is very important. The business must be accessible. Businesses often locate in industrial/business parks.

Where can I go for help?

The government offers lots of support and training to new businesses.

FÁS is the state training and employment authority. It operates extensive training courses provided at centres throughout the county. These services are tailored to the needs of regional and local enterprise. FÁS also provides an employment and recruitment service.

Enterprise Ireland is the state agency with responsibility for developing industry in Ireland. Their focus is on the development of industry by indigenous entrepreneurs and organisations.

The *County Enterprise Board* is responsible for the development of enterprise initiatives throughout a county. County Enterprise Boards offer financial aid and a mentor service. A mentor will give the new entrepreneur advice and guidance.

Leader Plus offers financial assistance to local development in rural areas. Leader Plus promotes rural development, offering financial aid to promotion of tourism, rural enterprise development etc.

Investigation of a local enterprise

Divide into teams and plan an investigation into a local business enterprise.

Step 1: Identify a range of enterprises in your local community.

Step 2: Identify an enterprise that interests you all. Discuss the various enterprises you have identified and choose one to investigate.

Step 3: Complete a brief background about the enterprise. You could use the following sources of information:
- **business website**
- **phone book (phone the business)**
- **family and friends**

Enterprise name:	
Contact name:	
Enterprise address:	
Contact number:	
Description of business:	

Step 4: Plan a visit to the enterprise to complete a more detailed investigation into this enterprise.

> ## Core portfolio item

ENTERPRISE PLAN
(300–600 words)
*Must be written in the future tense: you are planning for something you are **going** to do.*

Title of plan
What the plan is about.

_____

_____

Objectives
What you and your class plan to get from this activity.
Personal objectives

_____

_____

_____

_____

Group objectives

_____

_____

_____

Research

Areas you need to research in the order in which they need to be researched. Examples: permission from principal, suitable dates, suitable questions (see p.164), permission from parents, suitable transport if required, roles of each person in the group on the visit.

Analysis of research

*You must analyse each item you researched – you are now writing about something you have already done and in this section **only** you can write in the past tense.*

Action steps and schedule of time

What you need to do and when you plan to do it.

Time	Date	Task

Schedule of costs

Any income and costs involved in the visit. You may fundraise to pay for the visit. You may have photocopying, transport costs.

Income	€
Expenditure	€
Total surplus/deficit	€

Evaluation methods

This must link with objectives. How will you (personally) evaluate your contribution to the activity? How as a group will you be able to evaluate the success of the activity? Remember you have not yet completed the activity so you are identifying ways you plan to evaluate; this must be in the future tense.

Personal evaluation

Group evaluation

This plan can be submitted as a portfolio item so long as it does not link with any other portfolio item.

> IT: Use a word processing software package (e.g. Microsoft Word) to type up your plan. It should be typed in Times New Roman font, size 12. Make headings and subheadings stand out by using **bold** and *italics*.

Sample questions

The following are some sample questions you should ask on your visit. You should also use relevant Leaving Certificate subjects to formulate questions about aspects of your chosen enterprise.

- Describe the product/service you develop.
- Describe the roles of some of the employees in this business.
- What impact does the Single European Market have on your business dealings?
- How do you use information and communication technologies in your business?
- What education or training did you find important in developing your enterprise?
- How do you help the local community?
- What do you consider to be your strengths and weaknesses?
- Can you identify any opportunities or threats for your future?
- Would anybody in the business be willing to visit our LCVP class to talk to the group in further detail?

Once your team has completed the plan you can now visit the local enterprise. Use the following space to take down details of your visit.

Business enterprise investigated:

Main findings:

Evaluate the activity
Personal evaluation
What did you get from this activity? Did you learn information you did not previously know? Did you improve any skills?

Group evaluation

Have a discussion among group members. Did you work well together?

_____

_____

_____

_____

_____

_____

_____

Class evaluation

The class should discuss in an orderly manner each group's investigation of the business they investigated.

SWOT analysis

Use a SWOT analysis to identify what the enterprise is doing now and to help in identifying its future.

SWOT stands for:

S: Strengths – these are internal and present now. Example: Highly skilled employees.
W: Weaknesses – these are internal and present now. Example: a lot of debt (loans).
Strengths and weaknesses are internal. The business affects them and can change them.
O: Opportunities – these are external and are in the future.
T: Threats – these are external and are in the future. Example: New technology.
Opportunities and threats are external. They are affected by external factors and are therefore more difficult for us to control. Example: Competition

Complete this SWOT analysis on the business enterprise you investigated:

STRENGTHS	WEAKNESSES
OPPORTUNITIES	THREATS

Organising a visitor

When each group has completed their investigation they should be given the opportunity to report their main findings to the class. As a class you should decide on one enterprise you would like to hear more about. Once you have decided on a business enterprise you can organise a visit to the school by a representative from that enterprise.

Steps in organising a visitor

Step 1: Organise a class meeting (see p. 134).

Possible items to include on the agenda:
- minutes from last meeting
- suitable dates for visit
- delegation of jobs
- permission from principal
- contact with enterprise
- preparation of questionnaire
- photocopying questionnaire

- suitable room for visit
- organisation of IT equipment if required
- refreshments for visitor
- collection of a donation from each student to purchase a card and maybe a small gift
- presentation of the card and gift to the visitor at the end of the visit
- someone to meet the visitor at the door and bring them to the room
- AOB

Draw up your own class agenda.

AGENDA
Title:
Date:
Time:
Venue:
Chairperson:
Secretary:
Agenda
Minutes from last meeting

AOB (Any Other Business)
Signed: (Secretary)

The secretary should take the minutes of the meeting. It is very important to take the names of people who are to do each job and when they should have the job completed by.

MINUTES OF MEETING

Meeting topic:	
Date:	
Time:	
Venue:	
Chairperson:	
Secretary:	
Minutes on each item discussed	

Signed: (Secretary)

Once you have successfully completed the visit in you should complete a summary report on the visit.

Core portfolio item

SUMMARY REPORT
(300–600 words)

Prepared by

Title of report
What the report is about.

Terms of reference
Instructions given to the report writer.

Aims
Can be included in place of terms of reference. What you and your group want to get from the activity.

Group aims

Individual aims

Body of report

Divide the report into three or more sub-headings. There must be a logical sequence to summarise your main findings. You may decide to place paragraphs in order of importance or in chronological order, depending on the subject matter of the summary report. The use of numbered or bold headings and bulleted lists is recommended.

Subheading 1

Subheading 2

Subheading 3

Conclusions
Must link with aims and report content.

Group conclusions

Individual conclusions

Recommendations

Suggestions for future action. Recommendations might also include ideas for follow-on activities or describe how you might perform better in a future exercise.

Signed:

This summary report can be submitted as a portfolio item so long as it does not link with any other portfolio item.

> **IT:** Use a word processing software package (e.g. Microsoft Word) to type up your report. It should be typed in Times New Roman font, size 12. Make headings and subheadings stand out by using **bold** and *italics*.

Exam questions

Q1.

Business enterprise is very important for any area. Consider a business enterprise with which you are familiar.

(a) State the type of business involved (what the business does). State **three** enterprising characteristics the owner/manager possesses.

Type of business:

_____

_____

_____

Characteristics:

_____

_____

_____

(7 marks)

(b) Describe the study/training the owner/manager required for this position.

_____

_____

_____

_____

(4 marks)

(c) Carry out a SWOT analysis for this business.

(8 marks)

(d) Outline **three** benefits the area gains from having this business enterprise.

(6 marks)

Q2.
Consider a local enterprise with which you are familiar.

(a) Describe the product/service offered by this enterprise.

(2 marks)

(b) 'Coping with uncertainty' is a characteristic associated with enterprising people. Consider the enterprise described in (a) above. Outline **three** uncertainties that the people who run this enterprise might face.

(6 marks)

(c) In the case of each uncertainty described in part (b) above, set out in detail how each can be planned for.

(9 marks)

(d) You have been asked to investigate the services available in your locality for individuals and for business. You must write a report.

(i) List **six** separate headings/sections that would appear in the report.

(ii) Who would benefit from this report? Explain why they would benefit.

(8 marks)

Q3.

Your class has decided to organise a visit to a local enterprise. You are responsible for organising a meeting in this regard.

(a) List **four** steps you should take to organise the meeting.

(2 marks)

(b) Draw up an agenda for the meeting.

(10 marks)

(c) List **four** objectives the class might have for the visit.

(4 marks)

(d) How can an enterprise benefit a local community?

(3 marks)

(e) How should your peers evaluate your organisation of the meeting? List **three** items that they should comment on.

(6 marks)

Section B

CASE STUDY
(30 marks)

ELECT. LTD

Ruth Flynn is twenty-seven years old. She sat her Leaving Certificate nine years ago. She did not know what she wanted to do so she did not apply for college at that time. She began working in a local factory which suited her, as she did not wish to move away from home. At first Ruth worked on an assembly line in MPD Ltd, an electronics factory making car radios and other small electrical goods. Ruth's job was assembling part of the radio as the conveyor belt passed along. She worked in a unit with ten other workers. After three years she was promoted to supervisor of her section. This involved record-keeping on the items produced and planning the week's work for the unit with the production manager. Despite the extra responsibility and extra money that came with her job, Ruth was beginning to get bored and decided to go to college at night. Four years later she qualified with a degree in Business Administration.

The management in MPD Ltd recognised that Ruth had talents and abilities and she became assistant manager in charge of purchasing the raw materials. This involved travelling to meet suppliers and planning for what was needed and when it would be needed on a day-to-day basis. Many of the parts have to be bought from abroad. This has resulted in delays in the delivering of parts for MPD Ltd and other firms in related industries.

An opportunity arose for an agent in this country to handle the buying of these parts on behalf of several manufacturers. Ruth thought about it and decided that this was the way forward for her. It would suit her personally and business-wise. She set up her own company, ELECT. Ltd.

There were many decisions to be made and Ruth had to draw up an extensive business plan so that she would be able to begin her business. This involved market research in this country to establish who her potential customers might be and also to ascertain what their requirements might be. She also had to carry out research to establish who the suppliers were at present and who could be possible suppliers for new products for customers. She found her local enterprise board very helpful.

Because Ruth was setting up an agency she did not need a large manufacturing plant: instead, she is the middle person between the supplier and the manufacturer. Much of her work can, and is, done over the phone and the internet. ELECT. Ltd meets with its customers on a regular basis to plan a schedule of what is needed by them and when they require delivery. The customers must have confidence that ELECT. Ltd will supply what is required at the correct time.

Ruth initially employed one person in the office, and later on, a sales person who deals with the customers. Because much of the work is done via the internet, Ruth knows that it is important to have an up-to-date, user-friendly website. She spent considerable time and money developing the website when the company was set up and she updates it regularly. Because the use of the internet in business is expanding, Ruth believes there are many opportunities for her to develop her business.

1. State and explain briefly **three** advantages to Ruth of setting up her own business.

(6 marks)

2. Outline **three** major decisions Ruth will have to make to ensure that her business is successful.

_____

_____

_____

(12 marks)

3. Identify **three** personal and **three** business risks associated with business expansion.
    Explain the implications of each.

_____

_____

_____

_____

_____

_____

_____

_____

_____

(12 marks)

UNIT EVALUATION
Did you cover specific learning outcomes?

SPECIFIC LEARNING OUTCOME	COVERED (TICK)
6.1 identify a range of enterprises in the local community	
6.2 understand how an enterprise starts up and what support/ training is available	
6.3 describe the steps required to plan and carry out an investigation of a local enterprise	
6.4 use learning from relevant Leaving Certificate subjects to formulate questions about aspects of a local enterprise	
6.5 organise a visit to a local enterprise and invite appropriate speakers to visit the group in school	
6.6 carry out a SWOT analysis of a business	
6.7 report accurately on a visit by an entrepreneur to the classroom and on a class visit to a local enterprise	
6.8 compare and contrast information gathered on a group visit to a local enterprise	
6.9 describe a local enterprise with particular reference to products, services, markets and workforce	
6.10 understand and describe the different roles of adults working in a business environment	
6.11 describe the impact of the Single European Market on a specific enterprise	
6.12 describe and evaluate the use of information and communication technologies in a business enterprise	
6.13 understand the importance of education and training in the development of a business enterprise	
6.14 link the activities in this unit to learning in relevant Leaving Certificate subjects	
6.15 evaluate the success achieved and problems encountered in this unit.	

Does this unit and your learning experience link with any other Leaving Certificate subjects?

SUBJECT	HOW IT LINKS

What was your favourite part of this unit and why?

_____

_____

_____

_____

Did you encounter any problems during this unit? How could you overcome these problems in future?

PROBLEM	SOLUTION

| Unit 7 | **Local voluntary organisations and community enterprises** |

This unit introduces students to enterprises other than commercial businesses. Students are encouraged to find out how these enterprises are organised, how they are funded and how they contribute to local development. The outcomes of this unit can be achieved by a combination of classroom teaching, analysis of case studies, out-of-school investigations and invited visitors to the classroom. As part of this unit, it is recommended that students engage in a local study of 'My Own Place'. This unit should be integrated with Unit 1.

SPECIFIC LEARNING OUTCOMES
The student should be able to

7.1	identify the voluntary bodies that carry out community work in the locality	p. 188
7.2	describe the work carried out by a range of voluntary groups in the locality	pp. 189–192
7.3	understand and describe the different roles of adults working in voluntary community organisations	p. 204
7.4	organise a visit to a local community enterprise and/or invite an appropriate speaker to visit the group in school	pp. 194–207
7.5	use learning from relevant Leaving Certificate subjects to formulate questions about aspects of a community enterprise	p. 203
7.6	integrate information from a variety of sources to prepare a report, plan or presentation on an aspect of community development	pp. 193, 198–203 207–211
7.7	link the activities in this unit to learning in relevant Leaving Certificate subjects	p. 222
7.8	evaluate the successes achieved and problems encountered in this unit.	pp. 221–222

What is a voluntary organisation?

A voluntary organisation is a non-commercial organisation. Its main objective is to provide a service, not make a profit. The staff work voluntarily (without payment) to benefit and help a community.

Examples of voluntary organisations in your area may include:
- St Vincent de Paul
- Alone
- Red Cross
- Amnesty International
- Irish Wheelchair Association
- An Óige
- An Taisce

What is a community enterprise?

A community enterprise is also a non-commercial organisation. It helps support a community by providing services to local people. Community development organisations were established to assist and promote local business enterprise.

Examples of community enterprises in your area may include:
- FÁS
- County Enterprise Boards
- Leader
- Area Partnership
- GAA
- Tidy Towns
- Girl Guides
- Scouts
- Residents Association

Differences between voluntary organisations/community enterprises and business enterprises (see page 154)
- *Aim:* voluntary organisations and community enterprises are non-commercial. Their main aim is to provide a service. Business enterprises are commercial enterprises whose main aim is to make a profit.
- *Staff:* voluntary-organisation staff work for free. Business enterprise staff are paid.
- *Finance:* voluntary organisations and community enterprises are financed by grants, fundraising events. Business enterprises are financed by loans and investors.

Investigation

Identify the voluntary bodies that carry out community work in your locality.

You must investigate your locality and identify:

- **voluntary organisations**
- **community enterprises**

Step 1: Write down any of these organisations that you are aware of.

Step 2: Have a class discussion and write down any organisations that you did not know existed in your locality.

Step 3: Ask at home or in your community about organisations in existence.

Step 4: Check in the golden pages under voluntary organisations.

Step 5: Check the organisations' websites.

Step 6: Each person in class should take responsibility to find a contact name and number for one of these organisations.

TYPE OF ORGANISATION *VOLUNTARY OR COMMUNITY*	NAME OF ORGANISATION	CONTACT NAME AND NUMBER	STUDENT(S) RESPONSIBLE

Divide into groups of two or three. Each group should investigate an organisation that interests you.

How to find information when investigating:
- **website**
- **contact the organisation – phone, letter, e-mail**
- **talk to members**

INVESTIGATION WORKSHEET

Title of investigation

_____

Group members
Group leader

_____

Other members

1. _____

2. _____

3. _____

Group aims

_____

_____

_____

_____

_____

_____

Individual aims

_____

_____

_____

The group leader should delegate (divide) research to each group member (including themselves).

Possible areas to research:

- history
- services to our community
- how organisation is financed
- roles of adults in organisation
- role of a teenager in the organisation

TASK	NAME OF GROUP MEMBER

Your task

_____

Your findings

_____

_____

_____

_____

_____

Unit 7 – Local voluntary organisations and community enterprises

Now you have completed your part of the investigation you must report back to other group members. You should take brief notes on each member's findings.

SUMMARY OF GROUP FINDINGS

Evaluate the activity

Personal evaluation

What did you get from this activity? Did you learn information you did not previously know? Did you improve any skills?

Group evaluation

Have a discussion among group members. Did you work well together?

Class evaluation

Each group could now present findings to the rest of the class and get feedback on both the organisation and the group investigation. Note: in case any member of the group is absent every member should have notes on each area of the investigation so as to fill in for the absent friend. (IT: Use a presentation software package such as Microsoft PowerPoint to present your findings.)

Organisation

_____

Investigation

_____

Organising a visitor

After each group has presented their organisation the class should take a vote to decide on which group they would be interested in doing more research on.

This could be done by:

- show of hands
- secret ballot – write your choice on a slip of paper and hand it up to the teacher
- sign a sheet under the organisation's name

Organise a meeting to plan the visit

See page 134 for details on meetings.

Step 1: Draw up an agenda for a meeting.

Possible items for the agenda:

- **minutes from previous class meeting**
- **identify speaker**
- **delegate jobs**
  - **contact visitor**
  - **permission from relevant people**
  - **find suitable room for visitor**
  - **refreshments for visitor**
  - **questions and answers**
  - **meet visitor on day of visit**
  - **buy thank-you card**
  - **present thank-you card**
  - **collect money from class**
  - **present gift/donation to visitor**
  - **organise IT equipment**
- **behaviour expected when visitor comes to school**
- **plan for visit to be completed**
- **AOB**

Step 2: Make sure everybody in class has a copy of agenda.

Step 3: Appoint a chairperson.

Step 4: Appoint a secretary to take the official minutes of the meeting (everyone should also take their own notes). The secretary should write down the names of anybody who volunteers to do a job and when they will have the job done.

Draw up your own class agenda

AGENDA
Title:
Date:
Time:
Venue:
Chairperson:
Secretary:

Minutes from last meeting

AOB (Any Other Business)

Signed: _____ (Secretary)

MINUTES OF MEETING

Meeting topic:

Date:

Time:

Venue:

Chairperson:

Secretary:

Minutes on each item discussed

Signed: (Secretary)

Plan for visit

Core portfolio item

ENTERPRISE PLAN
(300–600 words)
*Note: Must be written in the future tense. You are planning for something you are **going** to do.*

Title of plan
What the plan is about.

_____

_____

Objectives
What you and your class would like to get out of the activity.
Personal objectives

_____

_____

_____

_____

Group objectives

_____

_____

_____

_____

Research

Areas that need to be researched prior to organising the visit.

Analysis of research

*You must analyse each item you researched – you are now writing about something you have already done and in this section **only** you can write in the past tense.*

Action steps and schedule of time
What needs to be done and where will you do it.

Time	Date	Task

Schedule of costs
Any income/costs involved.

Income	€

Expenditure	€
Total surplus/deficit	€

Evaluation methods

This must link with objectives. How will you (personally) evaluate your contribution to the activity? How as a group will you be able to evaluate the success of the activity? Remember you have not yet completed the activity so you are identifying ways you plan to evaluate; this should be in the future tense.

Personal evaluation

_____

_____

_____

_____

_____

Group evaluation

_____

_____

_____

_____

_____

_____

This enterprise plan can be submitted as a portfolio item so long as it does not link with any other portfolio item.

> IT: Use a word processing software package (e.g. Microsoft Word) to type up your report. It should be typed in Times New Roman font, size 12. Make headings and subheadings stand out by using **bold** and *italics*.

Questions to ask the visitor
Note: Your visitor will probably give a short presentation before you are given the opportunity to ask questions; make sure you do not ask a question covered in the presentation.

Use learning from relevant Leaving Certificate subjects to formulate questions about aspects of the community enterprise.

Q. What work does your organisation carry out in our locality?

A. _____

_____

_____

_____

_____

Q. What is your role?

A.

Q. How does your organisation differ from a business enterprise?

A.

Q. How is your organisation funded?

A.

Q. How can we help your organisation?

A.

Q.

A.

Q.

A.

Q.

A.

Q.

A.

Q.

A.

Prepare a summary report on the visit you and your classmates organised.

> **Core portfolio item**

SUMMARY REPORT
(300–600 words)

Prepared by
Your name.

_____

Title of report
What the report is about.

_____

_____

Terms of reference
Instructions given to you, the report writer; the purpose of the report.

_____

_____

_____

_____

Aims
Can be used in place of terms of reference.
What you and your class want to get from the activity.

Group aims

_____

_____

_____

_____

_____

Individual aims

Body of report

Divide your report into three or more subheadings. There must be a logical sequence to summarise your main findings. You may decide to place paragraphs in order of importance, or in chronological order, depending on the subject matter of the summary report. The use of numbered or bold headings and bulleted lists is recommended.

Subheading 1

Subheading 2

Subheading 3

Conclusions
Must link with aims and report content.

Group conclusions

Individual conclusions

Recommendations
Suggestions for future action. Recommendations might also include ideas for follow-on activities or describe how you might perform better in a future exercise.

Signed: _____

This enterprise plan can be submitted as a portfolio item so long as it does not link with any other portfolio item.

> **IT: Use a word processing software package (e.g. Microsoft Word) to type up your report. It should be typed in Times New Roman font, size 12. Make headings and subheadings stand out by using bold and *italics*.**

Exam questions

Q1.
Name **two** voluntary bodies that carry out community work in your area.

1. _____

2. _____

(a)   Select **one** of the bodies named above and draw up an agenda for a monthly meeting.

_____

_____

_____

_____

_____

_____

_____

(7 marks)

(b) Outline **three** benefits to local communities of voluntary organisations.

_____

_____

_____

_____

_____

_____

(6 marks)

Q2.
(a) Name **two** *voluntary* organisations in your area providing services to the local community.

_____

_____

(2 marks)

In the case of **one** of the organisations mentioned above, state **one** advantage *or* **one** disadvantage of (i) How it is run, and (ii) How it is financed.

(i) How it is run

Advantage:

_____

_____

Disadvantage:

_____

_____

(ii) How it is financed

Advantage:

Disadvantage:

(6 marks)

(b)   Describe briefly **three** differences between voluntary organisations and business enterprises.

(6 marks)

(c)   Explain why it is important to evaluate voluntary organisations.

(5 marks)

(d) Choose a voluntary organisation in your local area, other than the one detailed above, and write a short evaluation of this organisation.
You should include **four** distinct areas which you are evaluating.

(8 marks)

(e) Consider the location of an enterprise/organisation you are familiar with. Name the enterprise and outline **three** reasons why it is located in this place.

Name:

(7 marks).

Q3.

Your class has organised two visiting speakers to come and give a presentation to the class.

(a) List the organisations each speaker would represent. State the position each might hold within the organisation.

Organisation:

Position:

Organisation:

Position:

(4 marks)

(b) Outline **two** reasons why these speakers would be invited to the class.

(4 marks)

(c) Explain why it is important to evaluate the visits.

(4 marks)

(d) Name **one** person that holds a senior position in a voluntary organisation in your community. State what position he/she holds in the organisation.

(2 marks)

(e)   Name and explain **three** qualities this person has which help him/her in this position.

1.

2.

3.

(9 marks)

(f)   Write a brief report on the voluntary organisation. Set out the main body of the report using no fewer than **three** suitable headings. See pp.208–209

(12 marks)

Q4.

Voluntary bodies/community enterprises play an important role in the areas where they operate.

(a)   Name **two** voluntary bodies/community enterprises working in your area.

1. _____

2. _____

(2 marks)

(b)   Outline the work of **one** of the organisations you mentioned, stating who benefits from this organisation.

_____

_____

_____

_____

_____

_____

(6 marks)

(c)   Write a letter asking a speaker from one of the organisations to visit your class. Mention why you want them to visit.

_____

_____

_____

_____

_____

_____

_____

(11 marks)

(d)   Outline **two** ways you would evaluate this visit, stating **why** you have chosen each one.

(6 marks)

Audio visual questions
Link Modules Examination 2001
Trócaire (videotape available from LCVP Support Services)

Part 1

1.   Why was Trócaire founded?

2. Name two important aspects of Trócaire's work.

3. State **two** types of project which Trócaire supports.

Part 2

4. Why, in your opinion, does Trócaire provide training for local organisations?

5. Describe how Trócaire has expanded the focus of its fundraising activities.

6. Outline **two** benefits to Trócaire of introducing the 'donor's charter'.

Part 3

7. Do you consider Trócaire to be an efficient and socially responsible organisation? Give **three** reasons to support your answer.

8. Describe in detail why the director might be regarded as effective.

_____

_____

_____

_____

_____

Note:

The questions in part 1 and part 2 are based on the content of the video. Questions 7 and 8 of part 3 require students to draw from a wider knowledge and understanding required in courses of the link modules.

UNIT EVALUATION

Did you cover specific learning outcomes?

SPECIFIC LEARNING OUTCOME	COVERED (TICK)
7.1 identify the voluntary bodies that carry out community work in the locality	
7.2 describe the work carried out by a range of voluntary groups in the locality	
7.3 understand and describe the different roles of adults working in voluntary community organisations	
7.4 organise a visit to a local community enterprise and/or invite an appropriate speaker to visit the group in school	
7.5 use learning from relevant Leaving Certificate subjects to formulate questions about aspects of a community enterprise	
7.6 integrate information from a variety of sources to prepare a report, plan or presentation on an aspect of community development	
7.7 link the activities in this unit to learning in relevant Leaving Certificate subjects	
7.8 evaluate the successes achieved and problems encountered in this unit.	

Does this unit and your learning experience link with any other Leaving Certificate subjects?

SUBJECT	HOW IT LINKS

What was your favourite part of this unit and why?

_____

_____

_____

_____

Did you encounter any problems during this unit? How could you overcome these problems in future?

PROBLEM	SOLUTION

Unit 8   An enterprise activity

This unit provides students with the opportunity to put the skills they have gained in the previous units of the Link Modules into practice. It involves facilitating groups of students to plan, set up and run their own enterprise activities. Examples are: a community survey, a charity fund-raiser, publishing a newsletter or local tourist guide, organising a school event, setting up a mini-company to sell a product or provide a service. The form of enterprise project selected will depend on the aptitude and interests of the students, as well as the resources available to them in school and in the locality. It is essential in this unit that students are encouraged and permitted to take ownership of and responsibility for the enterprise projects they decide to pursue.

SPECIFIC LEARNING OUTCOMES

The student should be able to

8.1	work co-operatively with others to generate a range of ideas	p. 224
8.2	prepare a plan for the selected enterprise activity	p. 235
8.3	identify available resources to support an enterprise activity	p. 225
8.4	integrate information from a variety of sources including relevant Leaving Certificate subjects	p. 225
8.5	assess personal and group skills and identify possible training needs	pp. 226–230
8.6	identify and recruit consultants willing to advise on a selected enterprise activity	p. 226
8.7	understand the practical importance of market research and the marketing mix	pp. 230–235
8.8	be aware of the concepts of publicity and promotion	pp. 232–235
8.9	actively participate in group work in a variety of roles – owner, worker, team leader	p. 230
8.10	take responsibility to ensure that targets are reached	p. 238
8.11	participate in a review of group performance	pp. 242–244
8.12	review personal performance in an enterprise activity	pp. 250–251
8.13	prepare and present a written or verbal report on an enterprise activity	pp. 244–252
8.14	link the activities in this unit to learning in relevant Leaving Certificate subjects	p. 260
8.15	evaluate the successes achieved and problems encountered in this unit.	p. 261

ORGANISING AN ENTERPRISE ACTIVITY

The most important part of organising an activity is planning – 'failing to plan is planning to fail'. There are many steps involved in planning your enterprise activity, some of which include:

- **idea-generation**
- **research**
- **identifying available resources**
- **assessing your and your classmates' skills**
- **timetabling**

Each step is important to make sure you have a successful activity.

Idea-generation

Coming up with an idea that will be a successful enterprise can be difficult. We often refer to this stage as brainstorming. Remember the aim of enterprise is not always to make a profit; some enterprises exist to provide a service that is required in the community. Working alone read each of the headings below and brainstorm possible enterprise activities under each one. Many enterprise ideas stem from hobbies and interests; keep this in mind as you fill in the table.

ENTERPRISE ACTIVITY	EXAMPLES	YOUR IDEA
Provide a service	car cleaning, school bank/savings schemes, typing service – CVs for other students	
Make a product	school calendar, school magazine/newsletter, greeting cards, Christmas/Easter/Halloween decorations	
Organise an event	quiz, fashion show, school reunion, subject information afternoon for 3rd/4th-year students	
Do a course/ develop a skill	first aid, computers, photography, yoga	

After brainstorming alone have a whole class discussion to gather ideas from all of the class. Write three or four of the best and most achievable ideas on the board. Now it is time to vote on what enterprise activity you are going to aim for. Voting can be done in various ways:

- **show of hands**
- **secret ballot** – write your choice on a slip of paper and hand it up to the teacher
- **under the idea you prefer on the board write your name or an X: the idea with the most votes wins**

Identify available resources

Every enterprise needs support and help. The following is a list of people and resources that may assist you in your chosen activity.

- teachers
- parents
- board of management
- principal
- local business
- financial assistance
- community centre
- computer room
- books
- art room

From the list of resources and your own ideas identify those which would be able to assist your activity and state how.

RESOURCES		HOW THE RESOURCE COULD ASSIST
People:	teachers	
	parents	
	board of management	
	principal	
School facilities		
Local business		
Community		
Other		
Your own talents and attributes, e.g. Leaving Cert subjects that may help		

Identify people that could advise you in preparing and carrying out this activity:

CONSULTANTS	AREA OF EXPERTISE

Skills audit

You may not be aware of the skills you possess, individually or as a group. This skills audit allows you to identify your skills and may also highlight areas in which skills may need to be developed.

You are going to categorise the skills under three headings: personal, practical and interpersonal. Tick the boxes to rate yourself in each of the skill areas listed below. If possible give an example of where you demonstrated this skill in the last year.

PERSONAL SKILLS/QUALITIES	HIGH	MEDIUM	LOW	EXAMPLES
Honest				
Dependable				
Willing to learn				
Confident				
Determined				
Creative				
Show initiative				
Humorous				

PERSONAL SKILLS/QUALITIES	HIGH	MEDIUM	LOW	EXAMPLES
Friendly				
Organised				
Accept criticism				
Others				

TECHNICAL/PRACTICAL SKILLS	HIGH	MEDIUM	LOW	EXAMPLES
Writing letters				
Foreign language				
Computer skills				
Researching				
Managing money				
Numbers				
Generating ideas				
Designing/art				
Telephone skills				
Making things				
Cooking				
Report writing				
Others				

INTERPERSONAL/GROUP SKILLS	HIGH	MEDIUM	LOW	EXAMPLES
Work well with others				
Communicate well				
Lead others				
Allow others to lead				
Deal with conflict				
Listen to others				
Teach others				
Encourage others				
Get on/respect authority				
Speak in front of groups				
Others				

Personal profile
My skills are:

What I need to improve and how I can do this:

Team profile

This can be done in small groups or as a whole-class activity. First agree a list of strengths that the team has (team strengths) and then compile a list of the areas in which the team needs to develop skills (team weaknesses).

Team strengths:

Team weaknesses:

_____

_____

_____

_____

_____

_____

_____

Roles in the team

Each group activity is made up of team members taking on different roles. Each person's role is important; the listener is just as important as the organiser. Roles should be based on your skills, interests and career aspirations.

Some roles:
- **leader**
- **owner**
- **worker**
- **secretary**

Delegation

To make sure the work is all done and that it is done by the most qualified person it is important that work is delegated to different groups.

Each group should also have a team leader. *Example:* marketing, sales, production, liaising.

MARKETING

Marketing involves identifying, anticipating and satisfying customers' needs profitably.

Market research

Market research is an investigation of the potential demand for a product or service. Conducting market research involves gathering and evaluating information regarding your target market's (the people who will buy your product) preferences. Market research is important for the success of a product or service.

Desk research

This is researching information that is already available. *Examples:* statistics, research done by marketing companies (can be costly).

Identify methods of desk research that may be used to help with your enterprise activity. State how each could be used.

METHOD	HOW IT COULD HELP

Field research

Research your consumers using some of the following methods.
- questionnaire – these can be sent in the post or filled in face-to-face
- telephone interviews
- observing in the relevant stores

Identify methods of field research that may be used to help with your enterprise activity. State how each could be used.

METHOD	HOW IT COULD HELP

Marketing mix

Product: what you are going to sell. Every product should have a Unique Selling Point (USP): something that makes it different from other products on the market. How will it be packaged?

Price: what price to set in order to make sure costs are covered and profit made.

Place: where to sell and how to get it there.

Promotion: The promotional mix includes advertising, public relations, sales promotions, personal selling.

Each element of the marketing mix is equally important (see pp.232–235).
Think of a product that you are familiar with and complete a marketing mix on it.

MARKETING MIX FOR:
Product
Price
Place
Promotion

Prepare a marketing mix for your enterprise activity.

MARKETING MIX FOR OUR ENTERPRISE ACTIVITY:
Product
Price
Place
Promotion

Promotion

Promotion involves letting the customer know your product or service exists. Promotion can be carried out in the following ways:
- advertising
- public relations
- sales promotions
- personal selling

Advertising

There is a wide range of media that can be used to advertise. The method used depends on many factors, such as:

- advertising budget
- target market
- the message you wish to convey

ADVERTISING MEDIUM	ADVANTAGES	DISADVANTAGES
Television	picture and sound nationwide advert can be put on TV at the time your target market watches TV, e.g. toys advertised during children's TV	very expensive
Radio	can be nationwide not too costly	no picture
Newspapers	can be nationwide pick a paper your target market will read	often only black and white
Magazines	colour very specific to target market	
Outdoor: billboards, bus shelters, bus etc.	travelling advertisement colour	if people are rushing they may not notice advert

Identify types of advertising you could use for your enterprise activity.

ADVERTISING IDEAS FOR OUR ENTERPRISE ACTIVITY

Public relations

This is publicity through sponsorship. It is about promoting the good name of the enterprise. Often big companies pay famous people to promote their product. Identify some famous people that promoted a product or service:

PRODUCT/SERVICE	CELEBRITY

Another way to promote your enterprise is to sponsor an event. In your local community does any local business sponsor events or sports teams?

LOCAL BUSINESS	SPONSOR

Could you get local business to sponsor your enterprise activity?

LOCAL BUSINESSES THAT MIGHT SPONSOR OUR ENTERPRISE ACTIVITY

Sales promotions

This is a very common form of promotion that is affordable for small enterprises. It can include free samples, three for the price of two, buy one get one free. Identify a sales promotion campaign that you are familiar with:

ENTERPRISE NAME	SALES PROMOTION CAMPAIGN

Identify sales promotion ideas for your enterprise activity.

SALES PROMOTION IDEAS FOR OUR ENTERPRISE ACTIVITY

Personal selling
This involves using salespeople to directly sell your product or service. This is widely used in vehicle sales.

Plan your activity
You are now going to set out a plan for your enterprise activity. An enterprise plan should not be confused with a business plan (Unit 6).

Core portfolio item

ENTERPRISE PLAN
(300–600 words)
*Note: Must be written in the future tense. You are planning for something you are **going** to do.*

Title of plan
What the plan is about.

Objectives
What you (personally) and your classmates (group) want to get from this activity.

Personal objectives

Group objectives

Research
The research you will need to do before you can organise your activity. Examples: permission, people to contact for help, jobs to be delegated etc.

Analysis of research

You must analyse each item you researched – describe what you found out. You are now writing about the past (using past tense) about something you have already done.

Plan of action and schedule of time
What will you need to do in preparation for the activity, who will do it and when will it be done.

DATE	TIME	TASK AND WHO IS RESPONSIBLE

Schedule of costs
Any income/costs involved.

Income	€

Expenditure	€
Total surplus/deficit	€

Evaluation methods

This must link with objectives. How will you (personally) evaluate your contribution to the activity? How as a group will you be able to evaluate the success of the activity? Remember you have not yet completed the activity so you are identifying ways you plan to evaluate; this must be in the future tense.

Personal evaluation

Group evaluation

_____

_____

_____

_____

_____

_____

This enterprise plan can be submitted as a portfolio item so long as it does not link with any other portfolio item (other than the enterprise report).

> **IT: Use a word processing software package (e.g. Microsoft Word) to type up your plan. It should be typed in Times New Roman font, size 12. Make headings and subheadings stand out by using bold and *italics*.**

Review of activity
On completion of this activity it is important to evaluate the process.

Personal review
What was your contribution to the activity?

_____

_____

_____

_____

_____

Did you gain new skills and experiences?

What would you do differently?

Did you enjoy the activity?

Group review
Class discussion
What worked well?

_____

_____

_____

_____

_____

What would you do differently?

_____

_____

_____

_____

Questionnaire

1. **Did you achieve your aims? (Tick)**

   Personal   Yes [ ]   No [ ]

   Group   Yes [ ]   No [ ]

2. **Did you make a surplus or a deficit? (Tick)**

   Surplus   Yes [ ]   No [ ]

   Deficit   Yes [ ]   No [ ]

3. Did you work well as a team? (Expand)

4. Did you have any conflicts and if so how did you solve them?

Conflict

Solution

5. What was your role in the team?

6. Complete a team profile including new skills developed.
Team strengths

Report on the activity

Optional portfolio item

ENTERPRISE REPORT
(1000–1500 words)

Title

Prepared by

Prepared for

Date

Table of contents
Note: fill this in when your enterprise report is complete.

Topic	Page number
Summary	
Terms of reference	
Aims and objectives	
Body of report	
Planning	
Research	
Organising the activity	
The actual activity	

My personal contribution

Conclusion

Recommendations

Evaluation

Summary of contents
Summary of what this report contains.

Terms of reference
Instructions given to the report writer. The purpose of the report.

Aims
What you and your class wanted to get out of the activity.
Personal aims

Group aims

Body of report

Planning
Planning you did for the event.

Research

Link this with your planning – you researched the areas that required planning.

Organising the event

Write about the main areas that required organisation.

The actual event

What happened during the event – you are required to include a chart, table or diagram; it is a good idea to include a timetable of the activity in this section.

Timetable of the event

Optional: you may decide to use a chart or diagram instead.

TIME	ACTIVITY

My personal contribution

How did you contribute to organising the event and on the day of the event?

Organising the event

_____

_____

_____

_____

Day of the event

_____

_____

_____

_____

Conclusion

Link with aims.

Personal conclusions

_____

_____

_____

_____

_____

Group conclusions

Recommendations
Must be backed up by the contents of the report.

Evaluation
Personal evaluation
Did this activity draw on any of your Leaving Certificate subjects? Did you develop new skills?

Evaluation of event
Was the event a success? Did you work as a team? Did you raise money for charity?

_____

_____

_____

Evaluation of doing the report
Have you developed report-writing skills? Have you improved IT skills? Have you completed a portfolio item?

_____

_____

_____

This enterprise report can be submitted as a portfolio item so long as it does not link with any other portfolio item (other than the enterprise plan).

Exam questions

Q1.
Your class has been asked to organise a career exhibition in your school.
(a)   Draw up an agenda for a class meeting to organise the exhibition. Your agenda should contain at least **six** items.

_____

_____

_____

_____

_____

_____

_____

(9 marks)

(b) Name **two** categories of exhibitors who should be invited to attend.

(4 marks)

(c) A disagreement has arisen within the class about who does what on the day of the exhibition. Outline **three** steps that should be taken to resolve this dispute.

(6 marks)

(d) Why is evaluation important? Outline **two** ways the organisation of the exhibition could be evaluated.

(6 marks)

Q2.

Your class has been asked to organise a party in the school for the local senior citizens.

(a) Choose **one** activity and describe **three** of the main steps in planning it.

(6 marks)

(b) Draw up an agenda for a class meeting to organise the activity. Include **three** items on the agenda.

(7 marks)

(c) List **two** skills which are needed to chair this meeting.

(4 marks)

(d)   Write **four** questions that you should ask in evaluating this activity.

(8 marks)

Q3.

You have just completed fifth year in school. Together with four friends, you want to do something enterprising during the summer holidays. You would also like to make some money for next year, your last year in school.

(a)   How should you go ahead generating ideas for what you could do?

(1 mark)

(b)   Apply a SWOT analysis to the main idea for your enterprise.

(8 marks)

(c) Name **two** technical/practical skills:

Name **two** personal skills/qualities:

Name **two** interpersonal/group skills:

(6 marks)

(d) You have come up with an idea/project you think will work. Write out a short business plan for the project. Identify in your plan at least **four** key aspects of the project.

_____

_____

_____

(10 marks)

Audio visual question
Link Modules Examination 1998
Interact Ltd (Videotape available from the LCVP Support Service)

Part 1

1. When was Interact founded?

_____

_____

_____

_____

_____

2. Why was Furbo chosen as the location for the company?

_____

_____

_____

_____

_____

3. What are the key job areas in Interact?

Part 2

4. Why are young people attracted to the type of work available at Interact?

5. How does Interact ensure the quality of its websites?

6. What characteristics does Interact demonstrate that are common to successful businesses?

Part 3

7. What are the benefits of doing business on the internet?

8. How should Interact plan for the future? Give reasons for your answer.

Note:
The questions in part 1 and part 2 are based on the content of the video. Questions 7 and 8 of part 3 require students to draw from a wider knowledge and understanding required in courses of the link modules.

UNIT EVALUATION

Did you cover specific learning outcomes?

SPECIFIC LEARNING OUTCOME	COVERED (TICK)
8.1 work co-operatively with others to generate a range of ideas	
8.2 prepare a plan for the selected enterprise activity	
8.3 identify available resources to support an enterprise activity	
8.4 integrate information from a variety of sources including relevant Leaving Certificate subjects	
8.5 assess personal and group skills and identify possible training needs	
8.6 identify and recruit consultants willing to advise on a selected enterprise activity	
8.7 understand the practical importance of market research and the marketing mix	
8.8 be aware of the concepts of publicity and promotion	
8.9 actively participate in group work in a variety of roles – owner, worker, team leader	
8.10 take responsibility to ensure that targets are reached	
8.11 participate in a review of group performance	
8.12 review personal performance in an enterprise activity	
8.13 prepare and present a written or verbal report on an enterprise activity	
8.14 link the activities in this unit to learning in relevant Leaving Certificate subjects	
8.15 evaluate the successes achieved and problems encountered in this unit.	

Does this unit and your learning experience link with any other Leaving Certificate subjects?

SUBJECT	HOW IT LINKS

What was your favourite part of this unit and why?

Did you encounter any problems during this unit? How could you overcome these problems in future?

PROBLEM	SOLUTION

Blank calendars 5th year and 6th year

Teachers and students can plan a course of action, setting out:
- **when portfolio items are due**
- **modules to cover**
- **visits out**
- **visitor in**
- **use of computer room**

This should be done at the beginning of each academic year.

LCVP PROGRAMME FOR 5TH YEAR

Week beginning:	Week beginning:	Week beginning:	Week beginning:	Week beginning:	Week beginning:	Week beginning:
Work to be done:	Work to be done:	Work to be done:	Work to be done:	Work to be done:	Work to be done:	Work to be done:
Week beginning:	Week beginning:	Week beginning:	Week beginning:	Week beginning:	Week beginning:	Week beginning:
Work to be done:	Work to be done:	Work to be done:	Work to be done:	Work to be done:	Work to be done:	Work to be done:
Week beginning:	Week beginning:	Week beginning:	Week beginning:	Week beginning:	Week beginning:	Week beginning:
Work to be done:	Work to be done:	Work to be done:	Work to be done:	Work to be done:	Work to be done:	Work to be done:
Week beginning:	Week beginning:	Week beginning:	Week beginning:	Week beginning:	Week beginning:	Week beginning:
Work to be done:	Work to be done:	Work to be done:	Work to be done:	Work to be done:	Work to be done:	Work to be done:
Week beginning:	Week beginning:	Week beginning:	Week beginning:	Week beginning:	Week beginning:	Week beginning:
Work to be done:	Work to be done:	Work to be done:	Work to be done:	Work to be done:	Work to be done:	Work to be done:
Week beginning:	Week beginning:	Week beginning:	Week beginning:	Week beginning:	Week beginning:	Week beginning:
Work to be done:	Work to be done:	Work to be done:	Work to be done:	Work to be done:	Work to be done:	Work to be done:

Week beginning:	Week beginning:	Week beginning:	Week beginning:	Week beginning:	Week beginning:	Week beginning:
Work to be done:	Work to be done:	Work to be done:	Work to be done:	Work to be done:	Work to be done:	Work to be done:
Week beginning:	Week beginning:	Week beginning:	Week beginning:	Week beginning:	Week beginning:	Week beginning:
Work to be done:	Work to be done:	Work to be done:	Work to be done:	Work to be done:	Work to be done:	Work to be done:
Week beginning:	Week beginning:	Week beginning:	Week beginning:	Week beginning:	Week beginning:	Week beginning:
Work to be done:	Work to be done:	Work to be done:	Work to be done:	Work to be done:	Work to be done:	Work to be done:
Week beginning:	Week beginning:	Week beginning:	Week beginning:	Week beginning:	Week beginning:	Week beginning:
Work to be done:	Work to be done:	Work to be done:	Work to be done:	Work to be done:	Work to be done:	Work to be done:
Week beginning:	Week beginning:	Week beginning:	Week beginning:	Week beginning:	Week beginning:	Week beginning:
Work to be done:	Work to be done:	Work to be done:	Work to be done:	Work to be done:	Work to be done:	Work to be done:
Week beginning:	Week beginning:	Week beginning:	Week beginning:	Week beginning:	Week beginning:	Week beginning:
Work to be done:	Work to be done:	Work to be done:	Work to be done:	Work to be done:	Work to be done:	Work to be done:

EXAM TERMS

analyse	to study a problem in detail by breaking it down into various parts and examining possible relationships
apply	to bring knowledge or skills into use for a particular purpose
comment on	to express an opinion about something
compare	to examine two or more things in order to discover their similarities or differences
contrast	to show the difference/s between
criterion	a standard by which something can be judged or decided
characteristics	distinguishing qualities or attributes of an individual or object
define	to state the precise meaning of
describe	to give an account of a person, relationship, event, organisation or location
draft	to draw up a document, letter, report
evaluate	to find or determine the worth, value or significance of something; to assess or make a judgment
explain	to make clear in a detailed manner
identify	to show recognition of something
illustrate	to make clear by means of examples, charts, diagrams, etc.
indicate	to point out or state briefly
list	to write down a number of names or objects having something in common
mention	to refer to briefly
outline	to give a short summary of the important features of a subject
qualities	the distinguishing characteristics or attributes of an individual or object
suggest	to put forward an idea or a plan